PLAY THE GAME

Insider Strategies to Thrive In Your Early Career Without Compromising Ambition, Values, or Wellbeing

ELLEN RAIM *and* MARCIA HOMER

Acknowledgements

A huge THANK YOU to all the Gen-z early career professionals who helped with creation of this book. Reeve Berlinberg, Paige Creason, Tianna White, Jillian Berkowitz, Louisa Eckhardt, Aliza Lauter, Fiona McCann and Cameron Santiago we could not have done it without you!

Contents

Getting Grounded

Chapter 1

Introduction: Why You Need This Book

Hey there, if you're reading this, you're probably a young professional trying to figure out how to navigate the world of work. Maybe you're fresh out of college, or maybe you've been in the game for a couple of years and you're still feeling like an imposter in grown-up clothes. Either way, welcome to the club!

Let's agree: the workplace can be confusing. One minute you're crushing it with your innovative ideas, and the next you're wondering if you accidentally insulted your boss by not laughing at their dad joke. It's like trying to put together a puzzle when you don't have the box lid that shows the finished scene.

Every generation has faced its own set of challenges when entering the workforce. The difference? You're part of Gen Z, the most connected, tech-savvy, and socially conscious generation yet. You have the power to reshape the workplace in ways your predecessors could only dream of. But first, you need to learn how to play the game.

That's where this book comes in. Think of it as your personal guide to succeeding at work – minus the boring parts. We're going to break down everything you need to know to not just survive but thrive in your career. From understanding your Gen X and boomer bosses to navigating office politics that feel like a real-life version of "Among Us," we've got you covered.

Why should you trust us? Well, we understand both sides. We are part of the generation in charge and as former HR professionals we have worked with Gen Z employees who have come to us for help. We've also been where you are, so we have seen every mistake, and asked or heard every awkward question. Over the years, we figured out how to turn those cringe-worthy moments into stepping stones for success. Now, we're here to share those lessons with you, so you can skip the trial-and-error phase and go straight to being a boss (figuratively, for now).

In this book, we'll tackle questions like:

- How do I deal with a boss who takes credit for my work?

- What's the deal with "work-life balance" when my phone is always pinging?

- How do I ask for a promotion without sounding like I'm bragging?

- Is it too late to change my entire career path? (Spoiler: it's not)

We'll break it all down into bite-sized chunks, kind of like your favorite TikTok explainer videos, but with less dancing (unless that helps you learn – in which case, dance away!).

By the end of this book, you'll have:

- A better understanding of workplace dynamics

- Strategies for dealing with difficult situations.

- Tips for advancing your career.

- Insight into managing your work-life balance.

- The confidence to navigate office politics like a pro.

Remember, your career is a journey, not a destination. It's okay to feel lost sometimes – everyone does. But with this book in your back pocket (or more likely, on your Kindle), you'll have a roadmap to help you navigate the twists and turns.

So, are you ready to level up your career game? Let's start turning workplace challenges into opportunities for growth. Trust us, future you will thank you for it.

Tip: Don't just read this book – live it! Try applying one new tip each week and watch how it changes your work life.

Story Summary

- The workplace is confusing, but you're not alone.

- This book is your guide to succeeding at work.

- We'll tackle real issues you're facing.

- You'll gain strategies, tips, and confidence.

- Your career is a journey —make it an epic one!

Chapter 2

Gen Z Will Change the World: But Affecting Change Starts from Within

Let's face it: You're part of a generation that's poised to shake things up. Gen Z, your generation, has grown up in a world of rapid technological advancement, increasing social awareness, and global connectivity. You've got really innovative ideas, a strong sense of social justice, and the drive to make real change. We all know the working world needs exactly that kind of focus.

But here's the thing: making change isn't as simple as showing up on your first day of work with a list of demands and expectations. It's about understanding the system you're entering, learning to work within it, and then gradually building enough trust to reshape it from the inside out.

You might be thinking, "Wait a minute. Isn't that giving up or selling out?" Not at all. It's about being strategic. Think of it like this: if you want to redirect a river, you don't stand in the middle and try to push the water in a new direction. You start by understanding the current, then gradually alter the riverbed to guide the flow where you want it to go.

So, how do you start affecting change from within?

1. *Understand the current landscape.* Before you can change anything, you need to understand it. Take time to learn about your company's culture, processes, and the reasons behind them. Some things might seem wrong or outdated or inefficient to you, but there might be historical or practical reasons for their existence. Knowledge is power, and understanding the 'why' behind things will help you propose more effective changes.

2. *Build relationships and credibility.* Change doesn't happen in a vacuum. It happens through people. Build strong relationships with your colleagues and superiors. Show them that you're reliable, hardworking, and have the company's best interests at heart. When people trust you and value your input, they're more likely to listen to your ideas for change.

3. *Start small.* You probably have a laundry list of things you'd like to see done differently, but trying to overhaul everything at once is a recipe for resistance. Instead, start with small, achievable changes. Maybe it's offering a more efficient way to handle a specific task, or proposing to oversee a small sustainability initiative. Small wins build momentum and show that change can be positive.

4. *Be patient.* Rome wasn't built in a day, and neither will your ideal workplace. Change takes time, especially in large organizations. Don't get discouraged if things don't transform overnight. Keep gently offering to help with new ways of doing things, but understand that lasting change often happens gradually.

5. *Lead by example.* Want to see more environmental consciousness in your workplace? Start by bringing your own reusable water bottle and coffee cup. Want more inclusive language? Model it slowly in your own communications. Tip toe, but take a step or two.

6. *Collaborate across generations.* Your fresh perspective is valuable, but so is the experience of your older colleagues. Look for opportunities to collaborate with Gen X and Boomer coworkers. You might be surprised at how your different viewpoints can combine to create innovative solutions.

7. *Stay true to your values.* While it's important to work within the system, this doesn't mean compromising your core values. If something truly goes against your principles, speak up. Just do so respectfully and with well-thought-out alternatives.

Remember, you're playing the long game here. You have the potential to revolutionize the workplace, making it more inclusive, sustainable, and purpose-driven. Lasting change doesn't happen overnight. It happens through consistent effort, strategic thinking, and a willingness to work within the system even as you're working to change it.

You've got passion and the vision. It's important to develop patience and the strategy to turn that vision into reality. The work world needs your help. Start reshaping it, one small change at a time.

Tip: Find a mentor who has successfully implemented changes in your organization. Their insights can be invaluable in navigating the process of affecting change from within.

Story Summary

- You have the power to change the workplace.

- Understanding the current system is key.

- Build relationships, trust and credibility.

- Start with small, achievable changes.

- Be patient and persistent.

- Collaborate across generations.

- Stay true to your values while working strategically.

- You're playing the long game for lasting change.

Chapter 3

Understanding The Ones in Charge: The History of Gen Xers

To navigate today's workplace effectively, it's crucial to understand the people in leadership positions, many of whom are likely to be Gen Xers. Their upbringing and experiences are dramatically different from yours, which shapes their approach to work and management in ways that might seem puzzling or even frustrating to you.

Generation X, born roughly between 1965 and 1980, grew up in a world that prioritized independence and resilience over emotional support and constant supervision. Let's dive into what shaped their worldview:

The Latchkey Generation. Gen Xers were the original "latchkey kids." They came home to empty houses, let themselves in with a key often worn around their neck, and were expected to fend for themselves until their parents returned from work. This fostered a strong sense of independence and self-reliance, but also a certain emotional detachment.

Unsupervised Play. Unlike the structured playdates and constant adult supervision you might have experienced, Gen Xers were typically told to "go outside and play" and "come back when the streetlights come on." They roamed their neighborhoods in packs, creating their own games and solving their own conflicts without adult intervention. This taught them creativity, problem-solving, and social navigation skills, but also made them less accustomed to adult guidance and emotional support.

Physical Resilience. Gen Xers didn't have endless supplies of juice boxes and water bottles. They drank from garden hoses when thirsty. If they fell and scraped a knee, they were often told to "walk it off." This fostered physical toughness but also a tendency to downplay discomfort or needs.

Emotional Stoicism. Phrases like "stop crying," "suck it up," and "figure it out yourself" were common parenting tactics. This approach aimed to build resilience but often resulted in difficulty expressing or dealing with emotions, especially in professional settings.

Limited Technology. Gen Xers grew up with limited technology. They had to be creative in entertaining themselves and solving problems without the internet or smartphones. This fostered resourcefulness but also a potential skepticism towards constant connectivity and digital solutions.

Economic Uncertainty. Many Gen Xers came of age during economic recessions, fostering a strong work ethic and a "pay your dues" mentality. They often expect younger employees to prove themselves through hard work and perseverance.

How This Shapes Gen X as Managers:

1. *Emphasis on Self-Reliance.* Gen X managers often expect employees to figure things out independently. They may become frustrated with those who need constant guidance or reassurance.

2. *Discomfort with Emotions.* Having been raised to suppress their own emotions, Gen X managers may struggle with employees who are more emotionally expressive or who bring personal issues into the workplace.

3. *Skepticism Towards Social Issues at Work.* Gen Xers often view work as separate from personal life and may be uncomfortable when asked to take stances on social justice issues in the workplace.

4. *"Tough Love" Approach.* Like the fraternity "hazing" mentality, some Gen X managers believe that overcoming challenges without help builds character. They may not realize how this approach can be demoralizing for younger employees.

5. *Value on Face Time.* Having grown up without remote work technology, many Gen Xers place high value on being physically present in the office and may be skeptical of flexible work arrangements.

6. *Directness in Communication.* Gen X managers often prefer straightforward, no-nonsense communication and may be put off by what they perceive as overly sensitive or indirect approaches. They are also direct and to the point; and this may be off-putting for some.

The Gulf Between Generations: You can see how these traits might clash with Gen Z's expectations of a more supportive, inclusive, and flexible work environment. Where Gen X sees self-reliance, Gen Z might see a lack of mentorship. Where Gen X values stoicism, Gen Z values emotional intelligence and open communication.

Understanding these differences is key to bridging the gap. Remember, Gen X managers aren't trying to make your work life difficult – they're operating based on their own experiences and values. By understanding where they're coming from, you can better navigate your interactions and find ways to communicate effectively across the generational divide.

> *Tip*: When you're struggling with a Gen X manager's approach, try to frame your needs in terms of efficiency or problem-solving rather than emotional support. This can help bridge the communication gap.

Story Summary

- Gen X grew up with minimal supervision and high expectations of independence.

- Their upbringing emphasized physical and emotional toughness.

- As managers, they often expect self-reliance and may struggle with emotional expressions at work.

- Understanding these differences can help you navigate relationships with Gen X leaders.

- Frame your needs in ways that resonate with their values for more effective communication.

Chapter 4

Bridging the Generational Divide: Gen Z vs. Gen X Philosophies

In the previous chapter, we explored the Gen X mindset. Now, let's delve deeper into your generation, Gen Z, and how your upbringing and experiences have shaped your worldview and approach to work.

Gen Z: The Curated Generation

Born between the mid-1990s and early 2010s, Gen Z has grown up in a world dramatically different from that of Gen X. Interestingly, many of you were raised by Gen X parents who, perhaps in an attempt to compensate for their own "latchkey" upbringing, took a more involved approach to parenting.

Structured Childhood. Unlike the unsupervised play of Gen X, your childhood likely involved numerous organized activities:

- Scheduled playdates

- After-school lessons (music, sports, arts)

- Summer camps and enrichment programs

- Constant adult supervision and guidance

This structured upbringing has fostered skills in time management and multi-tasking, but may have limited opportunities for independent problem-solving and risk-taking.

Digital Natives. You've grown up with smartphones, social media, and constant connectivity. Technology isn't just a tool; it's an integral part of your life and identity.

Global Awareness. From an early age, you've been exposed to global issues and diverse perspectives through the internet and social media.

Defining Events and Issues. Your generation has been shaped by significant events and ongoing challenges:

- Born around 9/11, growing up with awareness of global terrorism

- The 2008 financial crisis and its aftermath

- Climate change and environmental concerns

- The rise of social movements
  (Black Lives Matter, Me Too, LGBTQ+ rights)

- COVID-19 pandemic and its global impact

- Rapid inflation and economic uncertainty

- Stagnant wages and rising costs of living, especially housing

These experiences have contributed to:

- A sense of uncertainty about the future

- Skepticism towards traditional institutions

- Strong desire for social justice and equality

- Concern about long-term financial stability

- Openness to non-traditional career paths and lifestyles

Gen Z Characteristics in the Workplace:

1. *Tech-Savvy.* You intuitively understand digital platforms and can quickly adapt to new technologies.

2. *Diversity-Minded.* As the most diverse generation in history, you value inclusiveness in all aspects of life and work.

3. *Social Justice Oriented.* You're passionate about addressing societal issues and expect companies to take stands on important matters.

4. *Mental Health Aware.* Your generation is more open about mental health issues and expects support in this area.

5. *Entrepreneurial.* Many of you have side hustles or aspire to start your own businesses, partly due to economic necessity and partly due to a desire for autonomy.

6. *Education-Focused.* You value ongoing learning and skill develop-ment, often through non-traditional means like online courses.

7. *Work-Life Integration.* You see work as part of your identity and expect it to align with your values.

Contrasting Philosophies

Now, let's look at how these traits contrast with Gen X philosophies:

1. *Work-Life Integration vs. Work-Life Separation.* Gen Z: You seek meaning and personal fulfillment in your work. Gen X: They often view work primarily as a means to support their personal life.

2. *Constant Feedback vs. Annual Reviews.* Gen Z: You prefer regular, ongoing feedback to improve continuously. Gen X: They're accustomed to more formal, less frequent performance reviews.

3. *Collaborative Work vs. Independent Problem-Solving.* Gen Z: You value teamwork and shared decision-making. Gen X: They often prefer to tackle problems independently.

4. *Social Impact vs. Financial Stability.* Gen Z: You prioritize making a positive impact through your work. Gen X: They often prioritize financial security and career stability.

5. *Flexibility vs. Structure.* Gen Z: You value flexible work arrangements and non-traditional career paths. Gen X: They often prefer more structured work environments and traditional career progression.

Bridging the Gap

While these differences might seem stark, remember that not all existing systems or people are inherently flawed. Many current structures have value, even if they need updating. Here's how you can start bridging the divide:

1. *Be Curious.* Ask questions about why things are done a certain way. There might be valid reasons you haven't considered.

2. *Share Your Skills.* Offer to help with technology or social media. This showcases your value while helping Gen X understand your capabilities.

3. *Seek Mentorship.* Express interest in learning from your Gen X colleagues' experiences. This builds trust and shows you value their knowledge.

4. *Explain, Don't Demand.* When you see a need for change, explain the reasoning behind your perspective rather than demanding immediate action.

5. *Start Small.* Propose small, manageable changes rather than overhauling entire systems at once.

6. *Be Patient.* Remember that change takes time, especially in established organizations.

7. *Show You Care.* Demonstrate genuine interest in the company's success and your colleagues' well-being. As Winston Churchill wisely said, "They don't care how much you know until they know how much you care."

8. *Educate Gently.* Help your Gen X colleagues understand your generation's perspectives and values. Share how global events and economic realities have shaped your outlook.

9. *Find Common Ground.* Look for shared values and goals. Both generations often value hard work, innovation, and making a difference.

10. *Be Open to Learning.* While you have much to offer, you also have much to learn from Gen X's experience and resilience.

Remember, the goal isn't to completely overhaul the workplace overnight. It's to create an environment where different generations can collaborate effectively, leveraging each other's strengths. By approaching the generational divide with curiosity, respect, and a willingness to learn, you can help create a more inclusive and effective workplace for everyone.

Tip: Next time you're discussing a workplace issue with a Gen X colleague, try sharing how your generation's experiences have shaped your perspective on the matter. This can open up meaningful dialogue and mutual understanding.

Story Summary

- Gen Z's upbringing and defining events have shaped a unique worldview.

- Key differences exist in how Gen Z and Gen X approach work and life.

- Economic realities and global issues have influenced Gen Z's career expectations.

- Bridge the gap through curiosity, skill-sharing, and open communication.

- Seek to understand before pushing for change.

- Find common ground and leverage each generation's strengths.

- Patience, mutual respect, and sharing perspectives are key to effective intergenerational collaboration.

Getting Hired

Chapter 5

Crafting Your Resume and Acing the Interview

As a Gen Z job seeker, you're entering a job market that's both exciting and challenging. While your tech-savviness and fresh perspective are valuable assets, it's crucial to understand that many hiring managers come from older generations. Let's start with creating a standout resume and then move on to interview tips.

Part 1: Crafting Your Resume

Your resume is often your first opportunity to make an impression. Here's how to make it count:

1. *Stick to Traditional Formats.* While video resumes might seem cool, it's better to use a traditional format. If you want to showcase your personality, consider a video cover letter as a supplement, not a replacement.

2. *Use Proper Grammar and Formatting.* This really does matter to more traditional generations. Proofread multiple times and have someone else review it as well.

3. *Keep it Concise.* Aim for one page unless you have extensive relevant experience. Use bullet points for easy readability.

4. *Tailor Your Resume.* Customize your resume for each job application. Highlight skills and experiences most relevant to the specific role.

5. *Use Action Verbs and Quantify Achievements.* Start bullet points with strong action verbs (e.g., "Developed," "Implemented," "Managed"). Include measurable results where possible (e.g., "Increased sales by 15%").

6. *Include Relevant Information.* List relevant coursework, internships, and projects if you're light on work experience. Include volunteer work or leadership roles in student organizations.

7. *Showcase Your Tech Skills.* Highlight your proficiency with relevant software and digital tools. If you have a digital portfolio or professional social media presence, include links.

Gen Z Tip: Create a master resume with all your experiences, then customize it for each application. This saves time while ensuring you're highlighting the most relevant information for each role.

Part 2: Acing the Interview

Once your resume has landed you an interview, here's how to make a lasting impression:

1. *Do Your Homework.* Research the company thoroughly (history, mission, recent news). Understand the role you're

applying for and how it fits into the organization. Look up your interviewers on LinkedIn if possible.

2. *Prepare Your Story.* Craft a concise, compelling narrative about your background and why you're interested in this role. Prepare specific examples that demonstrate your skills and problem-solving abilities. Think about how your unique Gen Z perspective could benefit the company.

3. *Dress Appropriately.* Err on the side of professional, even if the company has a casual culture. If unsure, ask the HR contact about the dress code.

4. *Mind Your Body Language.* Maintain good eye contact. Offer a firm handshake. Sit up straight and lean slightly forward to show engagement and enthusiasm.

5. *Communicate Effectively.* Speak clearly and avoid using too much Gen Z slang or jargon. Listen actively and ask thoughtful questions. Show that you can adapt your communication style to different audiences.

6. *Highlight Your Tech Skills (But Don't Overdo It).* Mention your comfort with technology but focus on how you can apply these skills to the job. If relevant, discuss any side projects or digital portfolios you've created.

7. *Address the Generational Elephant in the Room.* If appropriate, acknowledge your status as a young professional eager to learn. Highlight your ability to bring fresh perspectives while respecting established practices.

8. *Ask Insightful Questions.* Prepare thoughtful questions about the role, team, and company. Show genuine interest in the interviewer's experience with the company.

9. *Follow Up Professionally.* Send a thank-you email within 24 hours of the interview. Reiterate your interest and briefly mention a key point from the conversation.

10. *Be Prepared for Different Interview Formats.* Video interviews: Test your tech beforehand and ensure a professional background. For phone interviews, have your resume and notes in front of you. For in-person interviews, arrive early and bring a pad of paper to take notes.

The Importance of Not Ghosting

In today's job market, you might find yourself with multiple opportunities. However, it's crucial to maintain professional integrity:

- Never ghost an interview, even if you've accepted another offer.

- If you need to cancel, call or email as soon as possible to explain the situation.

- Remember, the professional world is smaller than you think – you may encounter these people again in your career.

- Burning bridges can harm your reputation and future opportunities.

- A simple, polite cancellation preserves relationships and leaves doors open for the future.

Gen Z Tip. Set a reminder on your phone to follow up after applying and to confirm interviews. This helps you stay organized and demonstrates your reliability to potential employers.

Story Summary

- Craft a concise, tailored resume with impeccable grammar and formatting.

- Prepare thoroughly for interviews, from company research to your personal narrative.

- Present yourself professionally in dress, communication, and body language.

- Highlight your tech skills relevantly and ask insightful questions.

- Follow up professionally and never ghost an interview.

- Remember, every interaction is a chance to build your professional reputation.

Remember, the goal is to showcase your unique Gen Z perspective while demonstrating that you can adapt to and thrive in a multi-generational workplace. Good luck with your job search!

Chapter 6

Navigating the Offer Negotiation Process

Congratulations! You've made it through the application process and interviews, and now you've received a job offer. But the process isn't over yet. Negotiating your offer is a crucial step in securing a position that meets your needs and values. Let's break down how to approach this process effectively as a Gen Z professional.

Understanding Your Worth

Before entering any negotiation, it's essential to have a clear idea of what's fair and reasonable to expect:

1. *Research Salary Ranges.* Use reliable sources like salary.com, Glassdoor, or PayScale to research salary ranges for your position and location. Be cautious of informal sources like TikTok spreadsheets or wikis, which may not provide accurate or contextual information. Likewise, asking your friends what they make may give you some rough information but it's not comprehensive.

2. *Consider Location and Company Type.* Salaries can vary significantly based on location, company size, and industry (e.g., tech vs. non-profit). Factor these elements into your expectations.

3. *Remember Your Entry-Level Status.* As a new professional, your starting salary may be lower than you wish it would be, it's because you are joining in an entry level position which means that the company needs to invest time and energy in your development. Focus on opportunities for growth and development alongside compensation.

Understanding Total Compensation

Your offer is more than just your base salary. A comprehensive compensation package includes:

1. *Base Salary.* Your regular paycheck amount.

2. *Health Insurance.* Often a significant part of your compensation, especially in the U.S.

3. *Retirement Benefits.* Such as 401(k) plans, potentially with employer matching.

4. *Bonuses.* Performance-based or annual bonuses.

5. *Stock Options or Equity.* Particularly common in startups and tech companies.

6. *Other Benefits:*
   - Work-from-home or hybrid options
   - Professional development or education benefits
   - Paid time off
   - Flexible schedules

Tip: If you're unsure about the value or importance of these benefits, do your research. Understanding these elements will help you evaluate the total package more effectively.

Negotiation Strategies

1. *Be Prepared.* Know your minimum acceptable offer and your ideal scenario. Have specific reasons why you're worth what you're asking for (skills, experiences, market rates). You don't need to lead a conversation with this, but be prepared to speak to it if necessary.

2. *Consider the Whole Package.* If there's limited flexibility on salary, consider negotiating for other benefits. Example: "While the base salary is lower than I hoped, would it be possible to include a professional development stipend?"

3. *Use Collaborative Language.* Frame your requests as solving a problem together, not as demands. Example: "It would make it so easy for me to say yes if the offer was [mention your desired change]."

4. *Be Professional and Respectful.* Remember, you're setting the tone for your future working relationship. Express enthusiasm for the role and company while negotiating. Put your best request forward when you negotiate. Companies are turned off by too much back and forth and requests that are out of the range they think is logical.

5. *Get It in Writing.* Once you've agreed on terms, ensure all details are included in your written offer.

Gender Considerations in Negotiation

It's important to acknowledge that gender can play a role in how negotiations are perceived. Research shows that women are often judged more harshly for negotiating assertively. Men may have more leeway in direct negotiations without negative perception.

For women navigating this process:

1. *Frame your request in terms of mutual benefit.* "I'm excited about contributing to the team. To perform my best, I'm hoping we can discuss [your request]."

2. *Use data to support your request.* "Based on market research for similar roles in our area, the typical range is [provide range]. Given my skills in [specific areas], I believe a salary of [your request] would be fair."

3. *Practice confident body language.* Maintain eye contact, use a firm handshake, and sit up straight.

4. *Consider negotiating beyond just salary.* Sometimes it's easier to negotiate for additional benefits or professional development opportunities.

5. *Seek mentorship.* Connect with successful women in your field for advice on navigating these conversations.

Remember, regardless of gender, as an entry-level candidate, it's often effective to use a collaborative approach: "I'm really excited about this opportunity. It would make it so easy for me to say yes if the offer was [mention your desired change]. Is there any flexibility there?"

This approach expresses enthusiasm while opening the door for negotiation in a non-confrontational way.

Remember:

1. *It's normal and expected to negotiate.* Most employers anticipate some back-and-forth.

2. *Be realistic.* As a new professional, your bargaining power may be limited, but that doesn't mean you can't or shouldn't negotiate.

3. *Consider the long-term.* Sometimes a lower initial salary with great growth potential can be more valuable than a higher starting salary with limited advancement.

4. *Consider other benefits.* If you can't get the salary you want, consider negotiating for other benefits such as more PTO or a performance review in 6 months with the potential for a raise.

5. *Practice your negotiation conversation with a friend or mentor.* Being prepared will help you feel more confident.

6. *Put your best foot forward.* When you make a counteroffer, make it your best request. Multiple rounds of negotiation or asking for something far beyond the company's range can sour the relationship or even lead to the offer being rescinded.

Tip: Keep the conversation positive. Focus on your excitement for the role and your desire to contribute to the company, not just on what you want from them.

Story Summary

- Research thoroughly to understand fair compensation for your role and location.

- Consider the entire compensation package, not just base salary.

- Use collaborative language in your negotiations.

- Be aware of potential gender differences in negotiation perceptions.

- Stay professional and get all agreements in writing.

- Remember, negotiation is normal and expected - approach it with confidence.

Negotiating your first job offer can feel intimidating, but it's an important skill that will serve you throughout your career. With preparation, professionalism, and a collaborative approach, you can navigate this process successfully and start your new job on the right foot. Remember, while it's important to advocate for yourself, it's equally crucial to maintain a positive relationship with your potential employer throughout the negotiation process.

Chapter 7

Onboarding: What to Expect and How to Prepare

You've successfully navigated the application process, aced your interviews, and negotiated your offer. Now comes a crucial phase in your new job journey: onboarding. While it might not sound as exciting as landing the job itself, onboarding is your gateway to understanding your new workplace, integrating into the company culture, and setting yourself up for success in your role. In this chapter, we'll explore what you can expect during onboarding and how you can make the most of this important transition period.

What to Expect

1. *Company Policies and Paperwork.* You'll likely be presented with an employee handbook and various documents to sign. Yes, it can be dry, but don't just skim through these. They contain valuable information about company policies, expectations, and your rights as an employee.

   Tip: Create a quick reference guide for yourself with key policies and deadlines you need to remember.

2. **Benefits Enrollment.** You'll need to sign up for health insurance, 401(k) plans, and other benefits. This is a big deal - these choices can have long-term impacts on your finances and wellbeing.

   Tip: Don't be afraid to ask for help in understanding your benefits options. HR is there to assist you, and making informed choices now can save you headaches later.

3. **Role and Team Introduction.** Expect to learn more about your specific role, your team's structure, and how your position fits into the larger organization.

4. **Tech Setup.** You'll likely get set up with necessary accounts, software, and possibly hardware needed for your role.

   Tip: Keep a record of your login information in a secure place. You'll thank yourself later!

5. **Company Culture Introduction.** Many companies use onboarding as an opportunity to introduce new hires to their values, mission, and culture. This might involve presentations, videos, or interactive activities.

6. **Networking Opportunities.** Onboarding often includes chances to meet colleagues, whether through formal introductions or more casual social events.

   Tip: Prepare a brief, engaging introduction about yourself. Practice it so you can deliver it confidently when meeting new colleagues.

How to Prepare and Make the Most of Onboarding

1. *Be Proactive.* Don't wait for someone to hold your hand through every step. Reach out, ask questions, and take initiative in getting to know your role and colleagues.

2. *Pay Attention to Policies and Benefits.* Even if it seems boring, give the employee handbook a thorough read. For benefits, don't hesitate to ask HR or a trusted colleague for help in choosing the right plans for you.

   Tip: Set aside dedicated time to review these documents. Treat it like studying for an important exam – your future self will appreciate it.

3. *Come Prepared with Questions.* Write down any questions you have about your role, the company, or your team. If they're not answered during onboarding, seek out the right person to ask.

4. *Network Strategically.* Use this time to start building relationships. Connect with fellow new hires on Slack or other platforms. Ask your manager for a list of key people you should meet in your first 30 days, then set up coffee chats or brief meetings with them.

   Tip: Keep a log of people you meet, including brief notes about their roles and any interesting points from your conversations.

5. *Make a Good First Impression.* In your initial meetings, focus on being curious and helpful. Ask people about their roles and how you might be able to assist them. Show that you're eager to learn and contribute.

6. *Engage Fully in Activities.* Whether it's a company scavenger hunt or a talk from a senior executive, participate enthusiastically. These activities are designed to help you integrate into the company culture.

   Tip: Even if an activity seems silly, approach it with a positive attitude. Your willingness to engage will be noticed and appreciated.

7. *Take Notes.* You'll be receiving a lot of information. Don't rely solely on your memory - jot down important points, especially about your role and initial tasks.

8. *Set Up Your Workspace.* Whether you're remote or in-office, take time to organize your physical and digital workspace in a way that will help you be productive.

   Tip: Don't be afraid to ask for ergonomic equipment if you need it. Your health and comfort are important for long-term productivity.

9. *Start Learning Company Systems.* Begin familiarizing yourself with the tools and software your company uses. The sooner you're comfortable with these, the smoother your transition will be.

10. *Be Patient with Yourself.* Remember, it's normal to feel a bit overwhelmed. You're not expected to know everything right away. Give yourself time to adjust and learn.

    Tip: Keep a "win" journal. Each day, write down one thing you learned or accomplished, no matter how small. It'll boost your confidence and show your progress over time.

Navigating Different Onboarding Experiences

Onboarding experiences can vary widely between companies. Some organizations have highly structured, engaging programs with group activities and executive welcomes. Others might take a more hands-off approach, providing you with documents and leaving you to figure things out.

If you find yourself in a company with a less comprehensive onboarding process, don't be discouraged. This is your opportunity to demonstrate initiative. Seek out the information and connections you need. Remember, your success in the role is ultimately your responsibility.

> *Tip*: Create your own onboarding checklist. Include things like "understand the company structure," "learn about key projects," and "meet with team members." This can guide your actions if the company's process is less structured.

Story Summary

- Be proactive in your onboarding process, don't wait for others to guide you.

- Pay attention to company policies and benefits.

- Come prepared with questions and take initiative in seeking answers.

- Network strategically, both with fellow new hires and key team members.

- Make a good first impression by being curious, helpful, and eager to learn.

- Engage fully in all onboarding activities, regardless of how they're structured.

- Take notes, organize your workspace, and start learning company systems.

- Be patient with yourself as you adjust to your new role and environment.

Onboarding is your launchpad into your new role. It's a time to learn, connect, and set the tone for your tenure at the company. By approaching it with enthusiasm, curiosity, and proactivity, you'll be setting yourself up for success in your new position. Remember, every interaction during onboarding is an opportunity to make a positive impression and start building professional relationships that will support your career growth. Whether your company offers a structured program or a more hands-off approach, your active participation in the onboarding process will demonstrate your commitment and help you integrate smoothly into your new workplace. Embrace this phase of your journey - it's the foundation upon which you'll build your professional future in the company.

Getting Along

Chapter 8

Your Role in the Big Picture: Understanding Why You Were Hired

As you settle into your role, it's crucial to understand not just what you're doing, but why you were hired in the first place. This understanding will help you align your efforts with the company's needs, demonstrate your value effectively, and set the stage for your long-term career growth.

Why You Were Hired

First things first: companies hire for specific reasons. When a position opens up, it's typically because:

1. *There's a new business need that requires additional manpower.*

2. *An employee has left, creating a gap that needs to be filled.*

In either case, the company is looking for someone to perform specific tasks and contribute to particular goals. While your personality and potential certainly played a role in getting you hired, at its core, the company needs you to fulfill certain responsibilities.

Tip: Take time to thoroughly understand your new role. If anything is unclear, don't hesitate to ask your manager for clarification. This shows initiative and helps you align your efforts with the company's expectations. If no job description exists, ask your manager to clearly define job responsibilities and expectations of the role.

Aligning Your Goals with Company Needs

Once you understand why you were hired, you can start thinking about how to align your personal career goals with the company's needs. Here's how:

1. *Excel in Your Current Role.* Focus on mastering the tasks you were hired to do. This builds trust and demonstrates your value.

2. *Show Initiative.* Look for ways to go "above and beyond" in your current responsibilities.

3. *Learn the Business.* Understand how your role fits into the larger picture of the company's operations and goals.

4. *Be Patient.* Remember, career growth takes time. Avoid asking about promotions too soon (e.g., "I've been here six months, when will I be promoted?").

Tip: Frame your desire for growth in terms of how you can help the company. Instead of asking, "When will I get promoted?", try, "What additional responsibilities can I take on to help the team and grow my skills?"

Demonstrating Your Value

Showing your worth to the company is crucial, but it's important to do so without coming across as impatient or entitled. Here are some strategies:

1. *Deliver Quality Work.* Consistently meeting or exceeding expectations is the foundation of demonstrating your value.

2. *Quantify Your Achievements.* Keep track of your accomplishments, especially those that directly impact the company's bottom line or key objectives.

3. *Build Relationships.* Your work doesn't exist in a vacuum. Building strong relationships across the organization helps others recognize your value.

4. *Be a Problem Solver.* Look for ways to improve processes or solve ongoing issues in your area of responsibility.

Tip: Keep a "win" journal where you record your achievements, big and small. This will be useful during performance reviews and when asking for new opportunities.

Communicating Your Achievements

While it's important to make your achievements known, there's a fine line between self-promotion and bragging. Here's how to strike the right balance:

1. *Regular Check-ins.* Set up recurring one-on-one meetings with your manager. Use these to discuss your work, challenges you've overcome, and the value you're bringing.

2. *Ask for Feedback.* In these meetings, also ask for your manager's perspective on your performance and areas for growth.

3. *Frame Achievements in Terms of Company Impact.* When discussing your accomplishments, focus on how they've benefited the team or company, not just on your personal success.

4. *Be a Team Player.* Acknowledge the contributions of others in your successes. This shows you're not just out for personal glory.

Tip: Practice the art of humble self-promotion. For example, "I'm excited about the project we just completed. The team worked really hard, and I'm proud that my contribution helped us finish ahead of schedule and under budget."

Developing a Long-Term Mindset

While Gen Z has a reputation for job-hopping, developing a long-term mindset can be beneficial for your career. Here's why and how:

1. *Skill Development.* Staying with a company allows you to develop deep expertise in your role and industry.

2. *Relationship Building.* Long-term relationships can lead to mentorship opportunities and strong professional networks.

3. *Company Knowledge.* Understanding the ins and outs of a company can make you an invaluable team member.

4. *Career Progression.* While it may take time, consistent performance in one company can lead to promotions and increased responsibilities.

Tip: Before considering a job change, weigh the pros and cons. Will starting over at a new company truly advance your career faster than growing within your current organization?

Remember, choosing to stay with a company is a personal decision. It should align with your values and long-term career goals. There's no one-size-fits-all approach to career progression.

Story Summary

- Understand that you were hired to fulfill specific needs of the company.

- Focus on excelling in your current role before seeking advancement.

- Demonstrate your value through quality work and problem-solving.

- Communicate achievements regularly, but with humility and team spirit.

- Build relationships across the organization.

- Develop a long-term mindset, weighing the benefits of staying versus changing jobs.

- Align your career decisions with your personal values and goals.

Your first job is the beginning of your professional journey, not the destination. By understanding your role in the bigger picture, aligning your goals with the company's needs, and demonstrating your value effectively, you set the stage for a successful and fulfilling career. Remember, growth takes time and patience. Focus on learning, contributing, and building relationships. Your efforts will be noticed, and opportunities for advancement will come. Embrace your role, make the most of where you are now, and keep your eyes on your long-term career goals. Your future self will thank you for the foundation you're building today.

Chapter 9

Building Trust:
Becoming a Valued Team Member

In today's interconnected workplace, your ability to build trust and become a valued team member can significantly impact your career trajectory. While delivering quality work is crucial, it's the relationships you forge that often set you apart. Let's explore how you can establish yourself as a trusted and valuable colleague.

The Trust Equation: Beyond Dependability

Trust in the workplace goes beyond simply being reliable. While consistently delivering on your promises is important, true trust has an emotional component. It's about creating a connection where your colleagues, especially your supervisors, feel that you genuinely care about their success and well-being.

Tip: Show interest in your colleagues as people, not just as coworkers. Learn about details of their lives outside of work and share yours.

Building Emotional Trust with Supervisors

Gen Z is known for being open and emotionally aware, which can be a great asset in building deeper connections. However, it's important to remember that older generations may have different comfort levels with personal disclosure. Here's how to navigate this:

1. *Be Genuine.* Show authentic interest in your supervisor's experiences and perspectives.

2. *Listen Actively.* Pay attention to what they share and refer back to it in future conversations.

3. *Offer Support.* Look for ways to make their job easier, even in small ways.

4. *Be Reliable.* Consistently deliver high-quality work on time.

5. *Show Discretion.* Respect confidentiality and avoid office gossip.

> *Tip:* Pay attention to your supervisor's communication style and try to match it. If they're more reserved, respect that boundary while still showing genuine interest.

Becoming a "Connector"

Employees who can build bridges between different people and departments often become invaluable team members. Here's how you can become a connector:

1. *Network Broadly.* Get to know people outside your immediate team.

2. *Share Information.* Pass along relevant articles or insights to colleagues who might benefit.

3. *Make Introductions.* Connect people who can help each other professionally.

4. *Volunteer for Cross-Departmental Projects.* This expands your network and knowledge base.

Tip: After meeting someone new, make a note of their interests or current projects. Follow up with relevant information or connections later to help them.

Integrating Relationship-Building into Daily Work Life

Building relationships doesn't have to be a separate task from your regular work. Here are ways to naturally incorporate connection-building into your day:

1. *Lunch Breaks.* Invite a colleague to join you for lunch.

2. *Coffee Runs.* Offer to grab coffee for a coworker or join them for a quick break.

3. *Before/After Meetings.* Arrive early or stay late for casual conversation.

4. *Collaborative Projects.* Use team projects as opportunities to showcase skills and build connections.

5. *Skill-Sharing Sessions.* Offer to teach a skill you're proficient in or attend others' sessions.

6. *Company Social Events.* Actively participate in company gatherings.

7. *Volunteer Events.* Join company-organized volunteer activities for a chance to connect in a relaxed setting.

Tip: Even in a remote work environment, you can build connections. Participate in virtual water cooler chats or suggest virtual coffee breaks with colleagues.

Maintaining Professional Boundaries

While building personal connections is important, it's crucial to maintain professional boundaries, especially as a Gen Z professional interacting with older colleagues:

1. *Avoid Oversharing.* Be cautious about sharing too much personal information too quickly.

2. *Respect Privacy.* Don't pry into personal matters unless invited to do so.

3. *Maintain Professionalism.* Even in casual settings, remember that you're still in a work context.

4. *Be Mindful of Hierarchy.* While many workplaces are becoming less formal, be aware of traditional power dynamics.

Tip: When in doubt, take cues from your more experienced colleagues about appropriate levels of personal disclosure.

Remember, building trust and becoming a valued team member is a process that unfolds over time. It's not about grand gestures, but rather consistent, genuine interactions that demonstrate your commitment to your colleagues and the organization. By integrating relationship-building into your daily work life, you can create a network of trust that will support your long-term career success.

Story Summary

- Building trust goes beyond dependability to include emotional connection.

- Become a "connector" by networking broadly and facilitating introductions.

- Integrate relationship-building into daily work activities.

- Maintain professional boundaries while building personal connections.

- Consistency and genuineness are key to becoming a valued team member.

As a Gen Z professional, your ability to build authentic relationships while respecting workplace norms can set you apart. By focusing on creating value for others, showing genuine interest in your colleagues, and consistently delivering quality work, you'll establish yourself as a trusted and invaluable member of your team. Remember, every interaction is an opportunity to strengthen your professional relationships and contribute to a positive work environment.

Chapter 10

The SCARF Model: A Framework for Workplace Interactions

Imagine this scenario: You're a young software developer who just joined a tech startup. You've proposed an innovative feature for the company's main product. Your idea could significantly improve user experience, but it would require changing some core processes. In the team meeting, your older, more experienced colleagues seem dismissive. Your direct supervisor, while intrigued, appears hesitant about presenting it to upper management. You leave the meeting feeling frustrated and undervalued.

This situation touches on all aspects of what neuroscientist Dr. David Rock calls the SCARF model. Understanding this model can transform how you navigate workplace interactions, especially across generational lines. Let's break it down.

What is the SCARF Model?

The SCARF model suggests that in social situations, including workplace interactions, our brains are constantly evaluating threats and rewards in five key areas:

1. Status

2. Certainty

3. Autonomy

4. Relatedness

5. Fairness

When these areas are challenged, it can provoke a defensive response, similar to facing a physical danger. Conversely, when they're reinforced positively, it can foster engagement and cooperation. Let's explore each element:

STATUS: *Your relative importance to others*

In the workplace, status isn't just about job titles. It's about feeling valued and respected.

Example: When your older colleagues dismissed your idea, it threatened your status, making you feel undervalued.

> *Tip:* Acknowledge others' expertise while asserting your own value. Instead of pushing your idea, you could say, "I'd love to hear your thoughts on this approach. Given your experience, you might see angles I haven't considered."

Remember: Everyone, regardless of age or position, wants to feel respected. Be mindful of how your actions might affect others' sense of status.

CERTAINTY: *Your ability to predict the future*

Our brains crave certainty. Ambiguity or uncertainty can feel threatening.

Example: Your supervisor's hesitation created uncertainty about the future of your idea and potentially your role in the company.

> Tip: When proposing changes, provide clear, detailed plans. You could say, "I've outlined a step-by-step implementation plan and potential outcomes. Would you like to review it together?"

Remember: You also crave certainty. When facing uncertain situations, break them down into smaller, more manageable parts to reduce stress.

AUTONOMY: Your sense of control over events

People like to have choices and feel they have control over their environment.

Example: Feeling like you couldn't move forward with your idea threatened your sense of autonomy.

> Tip: Instead of pushing for full implementation, you could ask, "Could we run a small pilot test of this feature? I'd be happy to lead it."

Remember: While you value autonomy, so do your colleagues and superiors. Always offer choices rather than demands.

RELATEDNESS: Your sense of safety with others

Humans are social beings. We naturally classify people as either 'friend' or 'foe'.

Example: The dismissive attitude of your colleagues threatened your sense of belonging in the team.

> *Tip:* Build relationships beyond work discussions. You could say, "I'd love to learn more about your experiences in the industry. Could we grab coffee sometime?"

Remember: In an era of increased remote work and digital communication, many Gen Z professionals report feeling isolated. Actively fostering relatedness can combat this loneliness. Organize virtual coffee chats, participate in team-building activities, or suggest in-person meetups when possible. These efforts to connect will benefit not just you, but your colleagues across generations, creating a more cohesive and supportive work environment.

FAIRNESS: Your perception of fair exchanges between people

Perceived unfairness can generate a strong threat response.

Example: You might have felt it was unfair that your idea was dismissed without proper consideration.

> *Tip:* Instead of labeling the situation as unfair, seek to understand. You could ask, "Could you help me understand the concerns about this approach? I want to learn how to better align my ideas with our goals."

Remember: What seems fair to you might not seem fair to others. Approach disagreements with curiosity rather than judgment.

Using the SCARF Model in Your Career

Understanding SCARF can help you navigate workplace interactions more effectively:

1. Before important interactions, consider how your words or actions might impact others in these five areas.

2. When you feel strongly reactive to a situation, use SCARF to identify which of your needs might be threatened.

3. In conflicts, try to address SCARF needs for all parties involved.

4. When working towards change (like diversity and inclusion initiatives), frame your approach in ways that don't threaten others' SCARF needs.

Remember, while you're passionate about justice and fairness, approaching these issues with patience and understanding will be more effective than making demands. By considering others' SCARF needs, you can advocate for change without triggering defensive responses.

Tip: Use the SCARF model as a tool for empathy and effective communication, not manipulation. The goal is to create a positive work environment for everyone.

Story Summary

- The SCARF model identifies five key areas that drive social behavior: Status, Certainty, Autonomy, Relatedness, and Fairness.

- Understanding SCARF can help you navigate intergenerational workplace interactions more effectively.

- Consider how your actions might impact others' SCARF needs.

- Use SCARF to understand your own reactions to workplace situations.

- When advocating for change, frame your approach to minimize threats to others' SCARF needs.

- Approach disagreements with curiosity and patience to build understanding across generational lines.

By understanding and applying the SCARF model, you can become a more effective communicator and collaborator in the workplace. This awareness will not only help you navigate your current role more successfully but will also provide a valuable framework for leadership as you advance in your career. Remember, creating a positive work environment isn't just about your own needs - it's about understanding and addressing the needs of those around you.

Chapter 11

Navigating Office Politics - A Gen Z Guide

Welcome to the complex world of office politics - a realm that's as crucial to your career success as your technical skills. For many Gen Z professionals, this can feel like navigating an invisible maze. But don't worry, we're here to help you decode the unwritten rules and thrive in your workplace.

Understanding Office Politics in the Modern Workplace

Office politics isn't about manipulation or backstabbing - it's about understanding human dynamics and organizational structures. It's an unofficial, but very real, system of relationships and power within your workplace.

> *Tip:* Think of office politics as a strategy game. Your goal is to advance your career and contribute to your team's success, all while maintaining positive relationships and your integrity.

Reading the Room and Unwritten Rules

In today's hybrid work environments, "reading the room" has become both more challenging and more critical. Here's how to develop this skill:

1. *Observe Before Acting.* Take time to watch how decisions are made, how disagreements are handled, and how ideas are presented. This is especially important in virtual settings where non-verbal cues might be harder to pick up.

2. *Leverage Technology.* Use collaboration tools and company social platforms to observe interactions and communication styles.

3. *Find a Mentor.* Seek out someone who can provide insights into the company's unwritten rules and culture.

4. *Start Small.* Begin with smaller contributions in meetings or projects, gradually increasing your participation as you become more comfortable.

Real-world Example: Sarah, a new marketing associate, noticed that while her team's Slack channel was casual and emoji-filled, emails to leadership were always formal. By observing this, she avoided the potential faux pas of sending a casual email to the CMO.

> *Tip:* Create a "workplace norms" note in your phone. Jot down quick observations about communication styles, decision-making processes, or unspoken rules as you notice them. This easily accessible reference can help you navigate workplace dynamics more effectively.

Balancing Ambition with "Paying Your Dues"

As a Gen Z professional, you're likely ambitious and eager to make your mark. However, it's important to understand the concept of "paying your dues" - not as a barrier, but as a growth opportunity.

Think of your career like learning to ski:

- You start on the bunny slopes (entry-level tasks), mastering the basics.

- As you improve, you move to more challenging runs (increased responsibilities).

- Eventually, you'll be tackling black diamond slopes (high-level roles), but only after you've built the necessary skills and experience.

Remember, each "run" teaches you valuable skills you'll need for the next level. Your goal is to master each level as quickly as possible, but rushing can lead to wipeouts!

> *Tip:* Frame your early career as an accelerated learning period. Seek out opportunities to learn from every task and every colleague.

Navigating Transparency vs. "Need to Know" Culture

Gen Z values transparency, but many workplaces still operate on a "need to know" basis for sensitive information. Here's how to navigate this:

1. *Respect Boundaries.* Understand that some information (like salaries or strategy) may be confidential for valid reasons.

2. *Ask Appropriately.* If you need information, frame your request in terms of how it will help you do your job better.

3. *Be Trustworthy.* Build a reputation for discretion. The more you're trusted, the more you're likely to be included in sensitive discussions.

Real-world Example: Alex, a junior developer, was curious about the company's expansion plans. Instead of asking directly, he expressed interest in how his current project fits into the company's long-term goals. This approach led to a productive discussion with his manager about the company's direction without breaching confidentiality.

Effective Communication Across Generations

Navigating generational differences is a key aspect of office politics. Here are some strategies:

1. *Adapt Your Style.* Be mindful of different communication preferences. Some colleagues might prefer emails, while others value face-to-face conversations.

2. *Mind Your Language.* Be cautious with slang or cultural references that might not resonate across generations or geographies if your company is global.

3. *Respect Experience.* While your fresh perspective is valuable, also acknowledge the experience of longer-serving colleagues.

4. *Bridge the Gap.* Look for opportunities to facilitate cross-generational collaboration, leveraging each group's strengths. Find opportunities to mentor longer-serving colleagues, if appropriate.

Real-world Examples:

The Shifting Support:

Emma's boss initially supported her presentation but then sided with the senior executive who was lukewarm about it.

How to Handle. Understand that your immediate supervisor may need to balance supporting you with aligning with senior leadership. This situation reveals that your boss may not always have your back, so keep this in mind for future interactions. Instead of feeling betrayed, view this as an opportunity to refine your work based on higher-level feedback. Ask your boss for a private debrief to understand the concerns and how you can improve.

The Name-Dropping Boss:

Jake's manager constantly referenced his connection to the CEO to enforce compliance.

How to Handle. While it's important to respect authority, it's also crucial to build your own credibility. Focus on delivering excellent work and gradually establishing your own relationships across the organization. Since your boss is focused on compliance, you may want to suggest that you and your boss discuss priorities regularly and set deadlines together so you can remain on track.

Disagreeing with Authority:

Zoe believed her boss's idea would lead to a suboptimal product, but wasn't sure whether to voice her disagreement or simply follow through with his plan.

How to Handle. In this situation, it's often best to express your concerns professionally. Frame your disagreement as a discussion, not a confrontation. Use phrases like, "I have some thoughts on how we might optimize this approach. Could we discuss it further?" Back up your view with data or solid reasoning, and always be open to understanding your boss's perspective. If after discussion, your boss still wants to proceed with the original plan, execute it to the best of your ability. You can document your concerns and the eventual outcomes for future reference or learning opportunities.

Remember, navigating office politics is a skill that improves with practice. Stay observant, be patient, and always act with integrity. Your ability to navigate these waters effectively will be a crucial factor in your long-term career success.

Story Summary

- Office politics is about understanding human dynamics and organizational structures.

- Observe workplace culture before acting, especially in hybrid environments.

- Balance your ambition with the need to gain experience and prove yourself.

- Navigate the tension between transparency and confidentiality with discretion.

- Adapt your communication style to bridge generational gaps.

- Always approach disagreements or challenges professionally and constructively.

As you navigate your career, remember that office politics is not about winning at all costs. It's about building positive relationships, understanding organizational dynamics, and positioning yourself to make meaningful contributions. By mastering these skills, you'll not only advance your own career but also contribute to a more positive and productive workplace for everyone.

Chapter 12

When and How to Ask for Help

As a Gen Z professional entering the workforce, you bring unique strengths and perspectives. However, you may find yourself wanting more instruction than your managers provide. This isn't a weakness—it's a natural result of your generation's experiences and the rapidly evolving workplace. The key is learning how to seek help effectively while demonstrating initiative and moving towards more confidence in approaching a project.

Understanding Your Need for Guidance

Several factors contribute to Gen Z's desire for more instruction:

1. *Preference for ongoing feedback.* You're used to quick, constant communication and may have thought you could expect the same in the workplace.

2. *Technological background.* While you're tech-savvy, humans are not wired as logically as technology. So, understanding how to operate in a work context may be less straightforward.

3. *Less work experience before your first professional job.* Due to the impact of recent global events, you may have had fewer opportunities for practical work experience than other generations of people by the time they entered the workplace.

4. *Emphasis on collaboration.* You value collaborative environments, which can translate to a desire for more question and answer with colleagues and superiors to get work done.

Recognizing when you need help is the first step. If you're unsure about priorities, deadlines, or processes, it's fine to seek guidance.

Strategies for Seeking Help Effectively

1. *Choose the Right Person.* Not all questions need to go to your direct supervisor. Identify knowledgeable colleagues who can assist with different types of queries.

   Tip: Ask your supervisor, "If I need a quick check-in or answer to something, who is the best person to ask? If it's you, how do you prefer to be contacted—email, Slack, phone, or text?"

2. *Time Your Requests.* Be mindful of your colleagues' schedules. If possible, batch your questions for scheduled check-ins rather than interrupting frequently.

3. *Frame Your Questions to Demonstrate Initiative.* Show that you've done some thinking on your own. Instead of asking, "How do I do this?" try, "I've started approaching this task by [your method]. Am I on the right track?"

Real-world Example: Marjorie, a new marketing associate, was given multiple assignments on Monday. On Tuesday, her boss asked for one task to be completed out of order by end of day. Sarah approached her boss and said, "Of course, I'll get this assignment done. Can we quickly review the rest of the week's activities and reprioritize them together given this change?" This approach showed initiative and problem-solving skills while seeking necessary guidance.

When to Figure Things Out on Your Own

While it's important to ask for help when needed, developing problem-solving skills is crucial for your career growth. Before asking for help, try:

1. Researching the issue using company resources or reliable online sources.

2. Breaking the problem down into smaller, manageable parts.

3. Attempting a solution and documenting your process.

If you're still stuck after these steps, you'll be able to show your supervisor the effort you've made when asking for help.

Balancing Detailed Instructions with Initiative

To request comprehensive instructions without seeming overly dependent:

1. *Start with a broad approach.* "Could you give me an overview of how this process typically works?"

2. *Follow up with specific questions.* "I want to make sure I understand the key points. Is [your understanding] correct?"

3. *Confirm next steps.* "Based on this, I plan to [your plan]. Does that align with your expectations?"

Real-world Example: John, a young engineer, was struggling with project deadlines because he was starting each task from scratch. His manager advised him to ask at the start of each project, "Who can I touch base with along the way to ensure I'm on the right track?" This approach helped John leverage existing resources and protocols, significantly improving his efficiency.

Building a Learning Mindset

View each task as a learning opportunity. Develop a system for retaining information, such as keeping a work journal or some other memory device. This can help reduce repetitive questions and demonstrate your growth.

Communicating Your Learning Style to Supervisors

Be upfront about your desire for guidance. So you don't threaten your manager's perception of your competence. You might say, "I'm eager to learn and contribute effectively. Would it be possible to set up regular, brief check-ins so I can ensure I'm meeting expectations and addressing any questions efficiently?"

Finding the Right Balance

Remember, everyone in the workplace is busy. It's important to find a balance between asking for validation of every step and trying to figure everything out yourself. This balance is key to your professional development.

Here are some strategies to help:

1. *Schedule regular check-ins.* Propose a consistent, but brief (15-30 minute) weekly or bi-weekly meeting with your supervisor.

2. *Be specific and prepared.* When asking for feedback, come with specific questions or areas you want to discuss to make the most of the time.

3. *Seek peer feedback.* Develop a network of colleagues who can provide informal feedback and guidance.

4. *Work towards self-regulation.* As you gain experience, try to evaluate your own work against clear criteria, gradually reducing your need to check in on the projects outside of key deliverables.

Remember, the goal is to become more independent over time while still maintaining open lines of communication with your team and supervisors.

Story Summary

- Understand why you might need more guidance as a Gen Z professional.

- Choose the right person and time to ask for help.

- Frame your questions to demonstrate initiative.

- Balance figuring things out independently with seeking necessary assistance.

- Communicate your learning style effectively to your supervisors.

- Work towards self-regulation while maintaining open communication.

- Remember that finding the right balance is crucial for your professional growth.

Mastering when and how to ask for help is a valuable skill that will serve you throughout your career. It demonstrates emotional intelligence, self-awareness, and a commitment to growth. By applying these strategies, you'll not only perform better in your current role but also set yourself up for long-term success and positive workplace relationships.

Chapter 13

Diversity, Equity, and Inclusion by Generations

In today's workplace, Diversity, Equity, and Inclusion (DEI) have become increasingly important topics. As a Gen Z professional, you likely enter the workforce with a strong commitment to these principles. However, you may find that older generations approach DEI differently. This chapter will help you navigate these differences and become an effective advocate for positive change.

Understanding the Generational Gap

As we discussed in earlier chapters, Gen Z and Gen X have different views of the world. Gen Z often views DEI as integral to the workplace, believing that companies should actively engage in social issues and pro-mote inclusive practices. In contrast, many leaders from older genera-tions may see DEI initiatives as separate from core business functions.

This difference isn't due to a lack of care but rather stems from different generational experiences and education. For example, many business leaders were taught to avoid any actions that might threaten the brand, including commenting on social issues. Understanding these perspectives is crucial for bridging the gap.

Effective Strategies for Advocating DEI

1. *Take Baby Steps.* Start with small, manageable initiatives that are less likely to meet resistance. For instance, suggest voluntary lunchtime training sessions on topics like neurodiversity or the significance of Juneteenth. As these efforts prove successful, you can gradually propose more comprehensive programs.

2. *Engage in Cross-Generational Mentoring.* Participate in or propose mentoring programs that pair younger and older employees. These relationships can foster mutual understanding and break down stereotypes, creating a foundation for more open discussions about DEI.

3. *Focus on Shared Values.* Identify common ground between generational perspectives on fairness, respect, and equal opportunity. Use these shared values as a starting point for discussions about DEI initiatives.

Engaging Allies

Finding supporters among older generations can significantly boost your DEI efforts. Look for leaders who demonstrate openness to new ideas or show interest in social issues. These allies can help translate DEI concepts in ways that resonate with other senior leaders.

Consider the approach taken by a group of Gen Z and young Millennial employees at one company. They identified senior leaders who were sympathetic to DEI causes and asked them to sponsor a DEI initiative. These senior sponsors then worked with the CEO to implement various programs, leveraging their established trust and influence.

Balancing Passion with Patience

While your passion for DEI is admirable, it's essential to balance it with patience and strategic thinking. Remember that company systems are primarily designed to ensure smooth operations and profitability. While progressive companies recognize the link between employee experience and company performance, many are still catching up.

Consider the following:

1. Recognize the value you're gaining from your current position, whether it's stability, good pay, benefits, learning opportunities, or great coworkers.

2. Evaluate whether it's worth investing time in patient, gentle advocacy for change, given these potential risks and other benefits.

3. Understand that lasting change often happens incrementally. Your ongoing presence and consistent advocacy can lead to significant shifts over time.

Pitfalls to Avoid

While passion is crucial, confrontational approaches can backfire. For instance, one employee sent a scathing email to the CEO, demanding immediate action on DEI initiatives. This approach branded the employee as a troublemaker, ultimately hindering DEI progress.

Instead, focus on constructive dialogue and collaborative problem-solving. Present DEI initiatives as opportunities for the company to improve and grow, rather than criticisms of current practices.

Conclusion: Building Bridges for a Better Workplace

As a Gen Z professional, you have a unique opportunity to bridge generational gaps and drive meaningful changes in your workplace. By approaching DEI with patience, understanding, and strategic thinking, you can be a powerful force for positive transformation.

Remember, the goal is not to overhaul company culture overnight, but to foster an environment where diverse perspectives are valued and included. Your ability to navigate these waters effectively — balancing idealism with pragmatism, passion with patience — will not only advance DEI initiatives but also contribute to your own professional growth and success.

By seeking to understand different generational perspectives, finding common ground, and advocating for change strategically, you can help create a more inclusive workplace for all. Your generation's commitment to DEI, combined with the experience and insights of older colleagues, can lead to powerful, lasting improvements in your organization.

Story Summary

- Understand the generational differences in DEI perspectives.

- Start with small, manageable DEI initiatives.

- Engage in cross-generational mentoring to foster understanding.

- Focus on shared values when discussing DEI.

- Identify and engage allies from older generations.

- Balance passion for DEI with patience and strategic thinking.

- Avoid confrontational approaches; focus on constructive dialogue.

- Remember that lasting change often happens incrementally.

Your dedication to DEI is a strength. By applying these strategies, you can effectively champion inclusion and equity, creating positive change while building strong professional relationships across generations. Your efforts today are laying the groundwork for the more inclusive workplaces of tomorrow.

Getting Things Done

Chapter 14

Mastering Work Hours and Prioritization

As a Gen Z professional, you're entering a workplace where expectations around work hours and task management might differ from your ideal. Mastering these aspects is crucial for your success and well-being. This chapter will help you navigate the sometimes tricky waters of work-life balance and prioritization.

Understanding Generational Differences

Gen X managers often view work as a significant part of life, frequently checking emails during off-hours and expecting similar dedication from their teams. As a Gen Z professional, you likely value a clearer separation between work and personal time. Understanding these different perspectives is the first step in finding a balance that works for both you and your employer.

It's important to recognize that many businesses operate on the assumption that salaried employees will work more than 40 hours a week. While this might not align with your ideal work-life balance, understanding this reality can help you navigate your career more effectively.

Effective Communication Strategies

1. *Setting Boundaries.* While you may need to be flexible with work hours, it's reasonable to protect your personal time, especially during weekends, holidays, and vacations. The key is communication.

2. *Proactive Communication.* Be clear about your availability and any potential conflicts well in advance. This shows professionalism and helps manage expectations.

    a. Example: Before a vacation, you might say, "I'll be completely off the grid next week. Can we identify someone to cover my projects in case anything urgent comes up?"

3. *Balancing Commitment with Personal Needs.* Demonstrate your dedication through the quality of your work and meeting deadlines, rather than always being available. This can help you maintain boundaries while still showing commitment.

Prioritization Techniques

Effective prioritization is crucial for managing your workload and meeting expectations. Here are some strategies:

1. *Stakeholder Involvement.* When juggling multiple projects— approach the relevant stakeholders: "I have several projects on my plate. Could we review them together to ensure I'm prioritizing correctly and setting realistic deadlines?"

2. *Handling New Requests.* When asked to take on new work, consider these responses:

a. "Yes." If you can accommodate it without compromising other work.

b. "No, I am sorry, I can't do that right now. We can look at a time in the future or I could try to help you find someone else." If it's clearly not feasible.

c. "Later." Provide a realistic short-term timeframe based on your current workload.

d. "I am happy to help but I need to check with my boss to understand how to fit it into existing priorities." If you're unsure or it conflicts with other priorities. Be sure and circle back with the stakeholder and confirm where it does land on your priority list.

3. *Regular Check-ins.* Keep stakeholders updated as your workload and progress change. This prevents surprises and allows for adjustments as needed.

Navigating Organizational Hierarchy

Understanding and respecting the organizational structure is crucial when managing your workload:

1. *Involve Your Boss.* Your direct supervisor should be your primary point of contact for prioritization. They can provide guidance and support, especially when dealing with competing demands from other groups or departments.

2. *Handling Non-supervisory Requests.* If colleagues who aren't your direct supervisors ask you to prioritize their work, it's okay to say, "Let me check with my boss to see how this fits with my current priorities. I'll get back to you soon."

3. *Building Trust.* Consistently delivering quality work on time builds trust with your supervisor and colleagues. This trust can give you more flexibility in managing your workload and time.

Potential Pitfalls and How to Avoid Them

1. *Misunderstandings About Availability.* Be clear about your off-hours availability. If you won't be checking emails during certain times, communicate this proactively.

2. *Saying No.* Turning down tasks can be uncomfortable, but it's sometimes necessary. Frame it positively: "I want to ensure I can deliver high-quality work on my current projects. Can we look at the timeline for this new task?"

3. *Balancing Multiple Stakeholders.* When different people are competing for your time, involve your supervisor in prioritization decisions. They can help navigate potentially sensitive situations.

Conclusion

Mastering work hours and prioritization is an ongoing process. It requires clear communication, proactive planning, and sometimes, compromise. By implementing these strategies, you can maintain a healthier work-life balance while demonstrating your value to the organization.

Remember, it's okay to advocate for your needs while also showing flexibility and understanding of business realities. Your ability to navigate these aspects effectively will contribute significantly to your professional growth and job satisfaction.

Story Summary

- Understand generational differences in work-hour expectations.

- Communicate boundaries clearly, especially for off-hours and vacations.

- Involve stakeholders in prioritizing tasks and setting deadlines.

- Respond thoughtfully to new work requests.

- Involve your boss in managing competing priorities.

- Build trust through consistent, quality work delivery.

- Be proactive in communicating and managing your workload.

By mastering these skills, you'll not only improve your current work situation but also set a strong foundation for your future career growth. Remember, finding the right balance is a journey, not a destination. Stay open to learning and adjusting your approach as you gain more experience in the workplace.

Chapter 15

Never Bring a Problem Without a Recommended Solution

As a Gen Z professional entering the workforce, you're likely eager to make a positive impression and contribute meaningfully to your organization. One of the most effective ways to do this is by adopting a solution-oriented approach to problems. This chapter will explore why this skill is not just beneficial, but a foundational workplace requirement.

Understanding the Concept

The idea of "never bringing a problem without a recommended solution" goes beyond simple problem identification. It's about taking ownership and initiative in your role. Many young professionals excel at spotting issues, but the real value lies in moving from "problem admiration" to problem-solving.

It's crucial to understand that continuous improvement isn't "extra work" - it's an integral part of every employee's job, regardless of their level. By adopting this mindset, you position yourself as a valuable team member who contributes to the organization's success.

> *Tip:* Adopt a mindset where you ask yourself, "When I see a problem, how can I prepare to solve it?" This proactive mindset will help you transition from problem-spotter to problem-solver.

Applying Existing Skills

You've been solving problems your entire academic career. Every essay, project, or exam that asked you to analyze a situation and propose a solution has prepared you for this aspect of professional life. The key is to apply these critical thinking skills to your workplace challenges.

For example, if you notice an inefficiency in a process, don't just point it out. Instead, think about how you would approach this problem if it were an assignment. What solutions can you propose based on your analysis?

> *Tip:* Try periodically asking yourself "what could we do better?" This practice will help you develop your problem-solving skills over time.

Presenting Problems and Solutions Effectively

In most cases, you won't need a formal presentation to discuss problems and solutions. Instead, focus on structuring a clear, concise conversation with the relevant stakeholders. Be prepared with:

1. A clear statement of the problem.

2. Your analysis of its causes and impacts.

3. Your proposed solution(s).

4. The reasoning behind your recommendation.

5. Any data or information that supports your analysis.

Remember, the goal is to demonstrate that you've thought the situation through and are presenting a well-considered recommendation, not just dumping a problem on your supervisor's desk.

Tip: Practice the "elevator pitch" version of your problem-solution presentation. If you can explain it concisely in 30 seconds, you'll be prepared for any opportunity to discuss it.

Handling Bad News

Sometimes, the problem you need to address is a mistake or a project going off-track. It's natural to feel worried or scared about having to tell your manager that there is a problem. But trying to ignore the problem because you are worried you will be judged is never the right solution. In these situations, you need to bring the matter to light quickly. Remember: bad news doesn't improve with age so waiting to make the issue known is not going to help. It's crucial to:

1. Acknowledge the issue promptly.

2. Take ownership, especially if you played a role in the problem.

3. Present your analysis of what went wrong.

4. Offer a plan to fix the situation and prevent similar issues in the future.

By addressing problems head-on and proposing solutions, you demonstrate maturity and reliability, even in challenging situations.

Tip: When delivering bad news, start by demonstrating you can be trusted to help solve the problem, deliver the bad news and your proposed solution, then end with another positive or forward-looking statement.

Balancing Urgency and Solution Development

While it's important to bring solutions, there are times when immediate escalation is necessary. In truly urgent situations – think "the building is on fire" level of urgency – it's appropriate to alert management immediately without a fully formed solution.

However, most workplace issues aren't this time-sensitive. For non-urgent matters, take the time to think through potential solutions before escalating. This approach shows respect for your manager's time and demonstrates your problem-solving capabilities.

> *Tip:* Develop a personal urgency scale from 1-10 to help you quickly assess situations. This can guide your decision on whether to escalate immediately or take time to develop a solution.

Common Pitfalls to Avoid

1. *"Problem Admiration".* Don't get stuck analyzing the problem without moving towards solutions.

2. *Assuming It's Someone Else's Job.* Remember, problem-solving is part of everyone's role.

3. *Bringing Half-Baked Solutions.* While you don't need a perfect solution, ensure your recommendation is well-thought-out.

4. *Fear of Proposing Ideas.* Don't let perfectionism prevent you from offering solutions. Your perspective is valuable, even if it needs refinement.

Real-World Example

Alice, a junior marketing associate, noticed that the team's project management software wasn't being used effectively, leading to missed deadlines. Instead of just complaining about the issue, she:

1. Analyzed how the team was currently using the software.

2. Identified key features that were being underutilized.

3. Created an outline on how to use these features effectively.

4. Proposed a brief training session for the team to her manager.

When she brought this to her manager, she didn't just present a problem of missed deadlines. She offered a concrete solution that could improve the team's efficiency. Her manager appreciated her initiative and implemented her suggestions.

Conclusion

Adopting a solution-oriented approach is not just about career advancement; it's a fundamental expectation in the professional world. By consistently bringing thoughtful solutions along with identified problems, you demonstrate your value to the organization and your readiness for more complex responsibilities. This approach will help you build a reputation as a reliable, proactive team member - someone who doesn't just point out issues, but actively contributes to solving them.

Story Summary

- Think proactively. Move from identifying problems to taking ownership and proposing solutions.

- Apply your skills. Use the critical thinking you've honed in school to tackle workplace challenges.

- Follow a process. Clearly define the problem, analyze it, brainstorm solutions, evaluate options, and recommend the best one.

- Handle bad news with maturity. Acknowledge issues, take responsibility, and present a plan to resolve and prevent them.

- Avoid common pitfalls. Don't get stuck analyzing problems or assume.

Adopting a solution-oriented approach isn't just about solving individual problems—it's about cultivating a mindset that will serve you throughout your career. Each problem you encounter is an opportunity to demonstrate your value and grow professionally.

Chapter 16

Time Management and Productivity Hacks

In today's hyper-connected world, mastering time management isn't just a nice-to-have skill—it's essential for career success and personal well-being. The modern workplace, with its constant stream of emails, messages, and notifications, presents unique challenges to staying focused and productive. This chapter will equip you with strategies to take control of your time and boost your efficiency in this fast-paced environment.

Understanding Your Time

Before you can manage your time effectively, you need to understand how you're currently spending it. Start with a time audit:

1. For one week, track all your work activities in approximately 30-minute increments.

2. Categorize these activities (e.g., meetings, focused work, emails, breaks).

3. Analyze the results to identify where your time is going.

> *Tip*: Use a time-tracking app like RescueTime or Toggl to make this process easier and more accurate.

You might be surprised to find how much time is lost to digital distractions or unproductive meetings. This awareness is the first step towards better time management.

Prioritization Techniques

With countless tasks vying for your attention, prioritization is key. Two powerful tools can help:

1. *The Eisenhower Matrix*: Categorize tasks as:

   - Urgent and Important (Do immediately)

   - Important but Not Urgent (Schedule)

   - Urgent but Not Important (Delegate if possible)

   - Neither Urgent nor Important (Eliminate)

2. *The 80/20 Rule (Pareto Principle)*. Focus on the 20% of tasks that will yield 80% of your results.

> *Tip*: At the start of each week, identify your top 3-5 priorities. Ensure these align with your team's and organization's goals.

Productivity Methods

Experiment with different productivity techniques to find what works best for you:

1. *The Pomodoro Technique.* Work in focused 25-minute intervals, followed by 5-minute breaks.

2. *Time Blocking.* Schedule specific blocks of time for different types of tasks.

3. *Task Batching.* Group similar tasks together to minimize context switching.

Tip: Use apps like Forest or Focus@Will to help implement these techniques and stay on track.

Digital Tools for Time Management

Leverage technology to boost your productivity:

1. *Project Management.* Tools like Asana, Trello, or Monday.com can help organize tasks and collaborations.

2. *Time-Tracking.* RescueTime or Toggl can provide insights into how you spend your time.

3. *Calendar Management.* Use Google Calendar or Microsoft Outlook to schedule your day and share your availability.

Tip: While these tools can be helpful, be cautious of app overload. Choose a few that genuinely improve your workflow rather than adding to your digital clutter.

Managing Distractions

In an age of constant notifications, managing distractions is crucial. You might want to:

1. Turn off non-essential notifications during focused work periods.

2. Use website blockers like Freedom or Cold Turkey during deep work sessions.

3. Create a dedicated workspace, even if working remotely, to minimize environmental distractions.

Tip: Communicate your "focus times" to colleagues so they know when you're available for quick questions and when you plan to carve out uninterrupted time.

Balancing Flexibility and Structure

While structure is important, the modern workplace often requires flexibility:

1. Create daily routines that anchor your workday (e.g., starting with a personal planning session, ending with a review of what you accomplished that day).

2. Be prepared to adapt your schedule for unexpected urgent tasks or collaborative needs.

3. Use time blocking, but leave some unscheduled time for spontaneous tasks or creative thinking.

Tip: Consider using the "1-3-5 rule": plan to accomplish one big thing, three medium things, and five small things each day.

Communicating Your Time Management

Effective time management also involves managing others' expectations:

1. Be clear about your availability and response times for different communication channels.

2. Learn to manage and set clear priorities (see the earlier chapter on this skill).

3. If you're overwhelmed, proactively communicate with your supervisor to reprioritize tasks.

Tip: If you decline a request, offer alternatives, or explain how it conflicts with current priorities. This shows you're considerate and strategic, not just saying no.

Continuous Improvement

Time management is an ongoing process:

1. Regularly review your strategies and adjust as needed.

2. Seek feedback from colleagues on your responsiveness and efficiency.

3. Stay open to new productivity tools and methods as they emerge.

Tip: Take time for a periodic "productivity self- review" to reflect on what's working and what isn't in your time management approach.

Real-World Example

Nate, a Gen Z marketing associate, struggled with balancing multiple projects and constant Slack messages. He implemented a system where he:

1. Used time blocking to dedicate focused hours to each project.

2. Set up "Do Not Disturb" times on Slack, communicating these to his team.

3. Batched email and Slack responses to two specific times each day.

4. Used the Pomodoro technique, a time management model, during his focused work blocks.

The result? Nate's productivity soared, and his stress levels decreased. His supervisor noticed the improvement in both the quality and quantity of his work, leading to more responsibilities and a potential promotion discussion.

Conclusion

Mastering time management is a crucial skill that will serve you throughout your career. By understanding your time, prioritizing effectively, leveraging productivity methods and tools, and continuously improving your approach, you'll be well-equipped to thrive in the fast-paced modern workplace. Remember, the goal isn't just to be busy, but to be productive in a way that aligns with your professional goals and personal well-being.

Story Summary

- Understand your time. Conduct a time audit to track and analyze where your hours are going.

- Prioritize smartly. Use tools like the Eisenhower Matrix or the 80/20 rule to focus on tasks that yield the biggest impact.

- Master productivity methods. Try techniques like Pomodoro, time blocking, or task batching to work efficiently.

- Manage distractions. Turn off non-essential notifications, use website blockers, and create a workspace that supports focus.

- Balance structure and flexibility. Plan your day with routines and time blocks but leave space for urgent or creative tasks.

Remember, finding the right time management strategy is a personal journey. What works for one person might not work for another. Be patient with yourself as you experiment with different techniques, and don't be afraid to adapt your approach as your role and responsibilities evolve. With practice and persistence, you'll develop a time management style that helps you excel in your career while maintaining a healthy work-life balance.

Chapter 17

Leveraging Your Tech-First Mindset

In today's digital-driven workplace, your innate understanding of technology is a powerful asset. This "tech-first" mindset - the instinct to turn to digital solutions for everyday tasks - sets you apart and can significantly contribute to your organization's efficiency and innovation.

Understanding Generational Tech Gaps

While you may navigate the digital world with ease, it's crucial to recognize that not everyone shares this comfort level. Older generations, including many in leadership positions, may approach technology with caution or even skepticism. This isn't a reflection of their capabilities, but rather a result of different experiences and learned work habits.

> *Tip:* Be patient when explaining tech solutions. What seems intuitive to you might be novel to others.

Key Areas of Gen Z Tech Proficiency

Your technological strengths typically include:

1. *App Discovery and Utilization.* You have a knack for finding the right digital tool for almost any task.

2. *System Integration.* You understand how different technologies can work together to streamline processes.

3. *Virtual Engagement.* You're adept at using tools to facilitate remote collaboration and team building.

4. *Advanced Web Research.* Your ability to quickly find and evaluate online information is unparalleled.

5. *Embracing Emerging Tech.* You're often early adopters of new technologies like AI.

Practical Applications in the Workplace

Your tech skills can transform everyday work processes:

1. *Streamlining Tasks.* You might find apps that automate routine work, save time and reduce errors.

2. *Enhancing Collaboration.* Your knowledge of virtual tools can improve team communication and project management.

3. *Improving Information Gathering.* Your research skills can provide quick, accurate data for decision-making.

4. *Automating Processes.* You might identify opportunities to use tech for automating repetitive tasks.

Real-World Example: An HR team member was tasked with creating an employee rewards program. She quickly found an online platform that allowed employees to collect "chits" redeemable for various gifts. This innovative solution, which older team members might not have discovered, effectively met the company's needs for both performance and tenure recognition.

Bridging the Generational Tech Gap

When sharing your tech knowledge:

1. *Focus on Benefits.* Explain how the tech solution solves a problem or improves efficiency.

2. *Be Patient.* Understand that what's intuitive to you may be challenging for others.

3. *Offer Support.* Be willing to guide colleagues as they learn new tools.

4. *Respect Experience.* Recognize that while you bring tech skills, your colleagues have valuable industry and organizational knowledge.

Tip: When introducing a new tool, create a simple step-by-step guide. This can help less tech-savvy colleagues feel more comfortable adopting the technology.

Reverse Mentoring Programs

Many organizations are implementing reverse mentoring programs, where younger employees share tech knowledge with senior colleagues. If your company offers this:

1. *Embrace the Opportunity.* It's a chance to showcase your skills and learn from experienced professionals.

2. *Be Respectful.* Remember, you're mentoring someone with significant career experience.

3. *Focus on Practical Applications.* Show how tech can make their job easier or more efficient.

4. *Be Open to Learning.* While you're teaching tech, absorb their insights about the industry and workplace dynamics.

If your company doesn't offer one, consider if it makes sense for you in your role to propose such a program. It could be a way for you to showcase your initiative and interest in the long-term success of the company.

The Human Element: Beyond the Tools

While your tech skills are valuable, remember:

1. *Critical Thinking is Key.* Technology is a tool, not a replacement for judgment and analysis.

2. *Understand Business Needs.* Ensure your tech solutions align with organizational goals and processes.

3. *Don't Overly Rely on Tech.* Sometimes, a face-to-face conversation is more effective than a digital solution.

> *Tip:* Before proposing a tech solution, ask yourself: "Does this truly solve the problem more effectively than existing methods?"

Staying Ahead: Continuous Learning in Tech

To maintain your tech edge:

1. *Stay Curious.* Keep exploring new technologies and their potential applications.

2. *Evaluate Critically.* Assess new tools for their practical business value, not just their "cool factor."

3. *Learn from Others.* Your colleagues might introduce you to industry-specific technologies you haven't encountered.

Communicating Your Tech Value

To effectively leverage your tech skills:

1. *Articulate Benefits.* Explain how your tech solutions contribute to business goals.

2. *Quantify Impact.* Where possible, measure the time or resources saved by your tech implementations.

3. *Be a Resource, not a Show-Off.* Offer your tech knowledge to help others, rather than to demonstrate superiority.

Real World Example

Grace, a young marketing associate, noticed her team struggled with coordinating social media posts across platforms. She researched and proposed a social media management tool that allowed scheduling and cross-platform posting. Initially, some team members were hesitant, but Grace created a simple guide and offered one-on-one help. Within a month, the team's efficiency improved dramatically, and Grace's initiative was recognized by leadership.

Conclusion

Your tech-first mindset is a valuable asset in today's workplace. By applying your digital native skills thoughtfully, respecting generational differences, and focusing on practical business applications, you can make significant contributions to your organization. Remember, the goal isn't to use technology for its own sake, but to leverage it to solve real business challenges and improve overall efficiency.

Story Summary

- You, as a Gen Z professional, bring unique tech proficiencies to the workplace.

- These skills include app discovery, system integration, and advanced online research.

- Effective application of tech skills can streamline processes and improve efficiency.

- Bridging the generational tech gap requires patience, focus on benefits, and respect for experience.

- Reverse mentoring programs offer opportunities to share tech knowledge and learn workplace wisdom.

- Balancing tech solutions with critical thinking and business needs is crucial.

- Communicating the value of tech skills effectively can lead to recognition and career advancement.

Your tech-first approach, when applied thoughtfully and communicated effectively, can set you apart as a valuable asset to your team and organization. Embrace your digital native status, but always keep the broader business context in mind as you apply your tech skills in the workplace.

Chapter 18

Navigating Organizational Dynamics: Understanding "How Things Work"

Guess what? Success isn't just about your individual skills and ideas. It's also about understanding and navigating the complex dynamics of your organization. This chapter will guide you through the often-unwritten rules of "how things work" in established companies.

Understanding Organizational Structure

Every organization has its unique structure, both formal and informal. While you might see a clear hierarchy on paper, the reality often involves intricate networks of influence and decision-making.

> *Tip:* Take time to study your company's org chart, but also observe how decisions are actually made. Sometimes, the person with the most influence isn't necessarily the highest ranking.

Decision-Making Processes

In larger organizations, decisions often involve multiple stakeholders. The RACI matrix is a good way to understand it. RACI stands for:

- Responsible: Who does the work?

- Accountable: Who makes the final decision?

- Consulted: Whose opinion is sought?

- Informed: Who needs to know the outcome?

Understanding your role in this matrix for different projects and work assignments can help you navigate decision-making processes more effectively.

> *Tip:* When starting a new project or assignment, you might ask your manager to clarify the RACI roles. This helps prevent misunderstandings later.

Keeping Your Boss Informed

There is one cardinal rule in any organization: never let your boss be surprised or out of the loop. This is because they may get updated information you do not have and keeping them in the loop keeps you on track. It also protects you in case someone questions aspects of the project and last, it keeps your boss from the embarrassing problem of having to say "I don't know" if they are asked about the work. So, regular, concise updates about your work, especially any challenges or potential issues, are important to your success.

> *Tip:* Ask your manager early on: "How do you prefer to receive updates from me? Email, Slack, scheduled check-ins? And how often?" This proactive approach demonstrates your commitment to effective communication and will allow you to keep your manager in the know.

Balancing Competing Interests

You may often find yourself in situations where different departments or decision-makers have conflicting priorities. It's rarely your job to make them agree, but rather to find a path forward that addresses key concerns.

Tip: When faced with competing interests, summarize each stakeholder's position in writing. This helps clarify the issues and shows you've considered all perspectives. Be sure and ask your manager if you need help re-prioritizing your workload.

The Pace of Change

If you're coming from a fast-paced academic environment or a startup, you might find the pace of change in larger organizations frustratingly slow. Remember, this often stems from necessary checks and balances, especially in regulated industries.

Tip: Instead of getting frustrated, use this time to thoroughly research and refine your ideas. Quality and thorough preparation often win over speed in established organizations.

Building Alliances and Influence

Networking within your organization isn't about manipulation; it's about building genuine relationships and trust. The more people know and trust you, the easier it becomes to get things done.

Tip: Make an effort to understand your colleagues' roles and challenges. Offering help or insights relevant to their work can be a great way to build positive relationships.

Adapting Your Communication Style

Different situations and audiences within your organization may require different communication styles. Learning to adjust your message and delivery so they can "hear you" and more easily accept your information can significantly impact your effectiveness.

> *Tip*: Pay attention to how senior leaders in your organization communicate. Mirroring their style (without losing your authenticity) can help your ideas resonate better.

Overcoming Fear of Leadership

Many young professionals feel intimidated by senior leadership, often to the detriment of their careers. Remember, leaders are people too, and most appreciate proactive, well-prepared team members.

> *Tip*: Don't avoid communicating just because management may make you nervous. If you're nervous about interacting with senior leaders, start small. Prepare a concise update on your current project and practice delivering it to a peer before sharing it with leadership.

Embracing Formal Processes

While some formal processes might seem unnecessary, they often exist for good reasons - regulatory compliance, quality control, or coordination across large teams. Accepting these as part of your routine can reduce stress and improve your efficiency.

> *Tip*: For recurring processes (like time tracking or regular reports), set up reminders or block time in your calendar. Making these tasks habitual will free up mental energy for more creative work.

Real World Example

When Noah joined a large corporation, he immediately scheduled a meeting with his new manager. "How do you like to receive information about what I'm doing?" he asked. "Email, Slack, one-on-one meetings? And how often would you like updates?" His manager was impressed by his proactivity, and they quickly established an effective communication routine. This not only helped Noah stay aligned with his boss's expectations but also positioned him as a reliable and considerate team member from day one.

Conclusion

Understanding "how things work" in your organization is a crucial skill that can significantly impact your professional success. While it might sometimes feel like navigating a complex maze, remember that every experienced professional has gone through this learning process. Stay curious, ask questions, and be patient with yourself as you learn to navigate your organizational landscape.

Story Summary

- Ask your manager about preferred communication methods and frequency. This will lead to establishing an effective communication routine.

- Decision making may be more complicated than you might think. Learn how to use RACI.

- Realize that hidden in the formal structure, there are a group of additional influencers. Learn who they are and get to know them.

- Watch how senior leaders in your organization communicate and mirror their style.

Remember, your fresh perspective and ideas are valuable, but they'll have the most impact when presented in a way that aligns with your organization's culture and processes. By mastering these organizational dynamics, you'll be better equipped to effect change and advance your career within the structure of your company.

Chapter 19

Work-Life Balance and Sense of Urgency

The modern workplace is experiencing a seismic shift. As Gen Z enters the professional world, they're bringing with them a radically different perspective on the role work should play in their lives. This chapter explores the tension between the desire for work-life balance and the traditional sense of workplace urgency, offering insights on how to navigate this complex terrain.

The New Work-Life Paradigm

For many Gen Z professionals, climbing the corporate ladder and taking time off to see the world or pursue a side hustle are equally valid life choices. This perspective marks a significant departure from previous generations' work-first mentality.

> *Tip*: Reflect on your long-term goals. How do you envision your ideal work-life balance? Understanding this can help you make informed career decisions. Talk with your manager ahead of time about work-life balance to avoid awkward situations where your vacation time may be denied.

The Generational Divide

While Gen Z values flexibility and personal time, older generations often prioritize work above all else. This fundamental difference can lead to misunderstandings and conflicts in the workplace.

Real World Example

The Weekend Work Dilemma– A company had a crucial project due on a Monday. The team, including several Gen Z employees, was told they might need to work over the weekend. When the call came on Sunday, one young worker didn't respond, later explaining he was "helping the senior manager understand when it's really necessary to work and to better understand work life balance." This resulted in a formal reprimand for insubordination.

Lesson: While advocating for work-life balance is important, it's crucial to understand when flexibility must yield to urgent business needs.

The Urgency Gap

The sense of urgency often differs between generations. This gap might stem from Gen Z's inexperience in an office environment – many Gen Z workers haven't yet witnessed the consequences of missed deadlines or unmet client expectations.

Real World Example

A junior employee was tasked with learning from a departing senior colleague. Despite having three weeks for the handover, the young worker consistently prioritized leaving work on time over these crucial knowledge transfer sessions. The result? Critical information was lost, and the junior employee faced repercussions.

Tip: Sometimes, short-term sacrifices are necessary for long-term success and stability in your role.

Navigating the Balance

While work-life balance is a worthy goal, it's essential to understand the realities of your industry and role. Here are some strategies to consider:

1. *Understand Your Industry.* Some sectors, like law and consulting, often require more sacrifice of personal time due to client demands. Some tech firms, especially those with a younger workforce, may offer more balance.

2. *Communicate Clearly.* If you need time off, communicate early and ensure there are no conflicting priorities.

3. *Be Available for Crucial Moments.* Understand the nature of your projects and be present for critical phases or deadlines.

4. *Leverage Flexible Options.* Many companies offer work-from-home days, summer Fridays, or hybrid schedules. Take advantage of these when available.

Bridging the Gap

1. *Work often comes first.* In large organizations and particularly early in your career, work is often expected to be your top priority.

2. *Build trust by demonstrating reliability during crucial periods.* This can lead to more flexibility later.

3. *Use your tech-savvy skills to your advantage.* Leverage your smarts to find efficient ways to complete tasks, potentially reducing overtime needs.

4. *It's ok to ask the "why" behind urgent requests.* That transparency may help you understand the need to do additional work.

The Long View

While it's tempting to prioritize short-term enjoyment, consider the long-term implications of your choices. Building a strong foundation early in your career can lead to more autonomy and balance later.

Remember, work-life balance isn't about equal time spent on work and personal life every single day. It's about achieving a harmony that allows you to meet your professional obligations while still pursuing personal fulfillment.

Story Summary

- You value work-life balance differently from previous generations, often prioritizing personal time and experiences.

- This can lead to conflicts in the workplace, as seen in the weekend work and knowledge transfer examples.

- Different industries have varying expectations – law and consulting often require more flexibility, while tech firms might offer more balance.

- Effective strategies include clear communication, understanding industry norms, and being available for crucial work moments.

- Flexible work options like remote work and hybrid schedules are becoming more common and that may allow for more flexibility.

- While advocating for balance is important, it's crucial to understand when work must take priority, especially early in one's career.

- Long-term career success often requires some short-term sacrifices.

By understanding these dynamics and finding ways to balance your needs with workplace realities, you can navigate your career more effectively. Remember, your approach to work-life balance may evolve as your career progresses. Stay flexible, communicate openly, and always keep both your personal and professional goals in mind.

Chapter 20

Mental Health And Work by Generation

The workplace landscape is shifting, and not just in terms of technology or job roles. A silent revolution is underway – one that's bringing mental health out of the shadows and into the forefront of workplace discussions. As a Gen Z professional, you're at the vanguard of this change, navigating a world where the stigma around mental health is slowly crumbling, but where generational divides still create friction.

The Mental Health Spectrum

Mental health isn't a binary state of 'well' or 'unwell'. It's a continuum that we all move along, influenced by work pressures, personal life, and societal factors. Understanding this spectrum is the first step in managing your mental wellbeing at work.

Tip: Regularly check in with yourself. Where are you on the mental health spectrum today? This self-awareness can help you take proactive steps when needed.

Generational Perspectives

1. The approach to mental health varies significantly across generations:

2. Baby Boomers and Gen X often view mental health as a private matter, something not to be discussed at work.

3. Millennials began breaking the silence, advocating for mental health awareness.

4. Gen Z, your generation, is pushing for open dialogue and comprehensive support.

This generational divide can create tension. While you might be comfortable discussing your anxiety or stress, your older colleagues or supervisors may find such openness uncomfortable or even inappropriate for the workplace.

Common Challenges for Gen Z

Several mental health challenges are particularly prevalent among Gen Z professionals:

1. *Burnout.* The always-on culture, coupled with high expectations, can lead to exhaustion and disengagement.

2. *Imposter Syndrome.* Feeling like a fraud despite your accomplishments is common, especially early in your career.

3. *Anxiety.* Workplace pressures, coupled with broader societal concerns, can fuel anxiety.

Navigating the Support Landscape

Many companies are expanding their mental health support, but navigating these resources can be tricky:

1. *Understand Your Benefits.* Review your company's benefits package. Many offer counseling services or Employee Assistance Programs (EAPs).

2. *Approach HR.* Don't hesitate to ask HR about available mental health resources. It's their job to help you understand and utilize your benefits.

3. *Utilize Digital Tools.* Many apps and online platforms offer mental health support, from meditation guides to therapy sessions.

Tip: When approaching HR, frame your questions in terms of wanting to understand all available resources for employee wellbeing. This approach can help alleviate any potential stigma.

Creating a Mentally Healthy Work Environment

While systemic changes often need to come from the top, you can take steps to foster a supportive atmosphere:

1. *Lead by Example.* Be open about prioritizing your mental health. This can encourage others to do the same.

2. *Set Boundaries.* Establish clear work-life boundaries and respect others' boundaries too.

3. *Practice Empathy.* Everyone struggles sometimes. A little understanding can go a long way.

Balancing Openness and Privacy

While Gen Z generally favors openness about mental health, it's important to consider your workplace culture and personal comfort level:

1. *Gauge the Environment.* Observe how mental health is discussed in your workplace before deciding how much to share.

2. *Start Small.* You don't need to divulge everything. Starting with general conversations about stress management is enough to open the door to deeper solutions..

3. *Know Your Rights.* Familiarize yourself with legal protections regarding mental health in the workplace.

The Role of Self-Care

Ultimately, managing your mental health is a personal responsibility. Here are some strategies:

1. *Prioritize Sleep.* Good sleep is foundational to mental health.

2. *Exercise Regularly.* Physical activity is a powerful mood booster and stress reliever.

3. *Practice Mindfulness.* Techniques like meditation can help manage stress and anxiety.

4. *Seek Professional Help.* If you're struggling, don't hesitate to consult a mental health professional.

The Future of Workplace Mental Health

As Gen Z continues to enter the workforce, the conversation around mental health is likely to evolve. Your generation's openness and advocacy can drive positive changes, making workplaces more supportive and understanding of mental health needs.

Remember, taking care of your mental health isn't selfish or unprofessional – it's essential for your long-term success and wellbeing. By prioritizing your mental health and gently advocating for supportive policies, you're not just helping yourself, but potentially creating a better work environment for everyone.

Story Summary

- Mental health awareness in the workplace is growing, with you and your peers leading the charge for openness and support.

- Generational differences exist in approaching mental health, with older generations often viewing it as a private matter.

- Common mental health challenges for Gen Z include burnout, imposter syndrome, and anxiety.

- Understanding and utilizing available mental health resources, including company benefits and digital tools, is crucial.

- Creating a supportive work environment involves setting boundaries, practicing empathy, and leading by example.

- Balancing openness about mental health with privacy considerations is important in the workplace.

- Self-care strategies, including sleep, exercise, and mindfulness, are essential for maintaining mental wellbeing.

- If a job consistently compromises your mental health; it might be a sign to explore other opportunities.

By prioritizing your mental health and advocating for supportive policies, you're contributing to a workplace culture that values well-being alongside productivity. Remember, a mentally healthy workforce is a more engaged, creative, and resilient one.

Chapter 21

Handling Mistakes, Failures, and Setbacks

In the grand tapestry of your career, not every thread will be perfectly woven. Mistakes, failures, and setbacks are not just inevitable; they're essential components of professional growth. How you handle these challenges can often be more defining than your successes. This chapter will equip you with strategies to turn these potential career stumbling blocks into stepping stones.

The Anatomy of a Mistake

Everyone makes mistakes. It's how you deal with them that sets you apart. Here's a five-step process to handle mistakes effectively:

1. *Come up With a Fix to the Problem.* Your first priority should be damage control. Identify what went wrong and outline immediate steps to correct it.

2. *Inform and Propose.* Communicate the issue to your boss, along with a proposed solution.

3. *Follow Through.* Stay with the problem until it's resolved.

4. *Learn and Prevent.* Analyze what led to the mistake and how you can prevent similar issues in the future both personally and at a company level.

5. *Continuously Improve.* Consider if this mistake highlights any systemic issues that could be addressed or redesigned on a broader scale.

> *Tip:* When informing your boss about a mistake, lead with the solution. For example, "I noticed an error in the report. I've already started correcting it and estimate it will be fixed by end of day. Here's my plan..."

Navigating Setbacks

Setbacks often come in the form of missed promotions or unsuccessful job applications. Remember, career paths are rarely straight lines. Here's how to handle these situations:

1. *Be Patient.* Understand that career progression isn't always about time served.

2. *Seek Feedback.* Ask how you can improve for future opportunities. Frame it as a desire to grow your skills.

3. *Develop Skills.* Work on building the experience that made another candidate more suitable.

> *Tip:* When seeking feedback, try: "I'm committed to growing in my role. Could you share any insights on areas where I could develop to become a stronger candidate for future opportunities?"

Overcoming Failures

Professional exam failures, like the CPA or Bar exam, can be particularly challenging. Here's how to approach these situations:

1. *Self-Reflect.* Use this as an opportunity to reassess your goals and commitment to your chosen path. It's ok to feel sad. But don't let this sadness overtake you.

2. *Analyze.* Understand why you didn't pass. Was it content knowledge, test-taking strategy, or time management?

3. *Plan.* Create a structured study plan addressing your weak areas.

4. *Persist.* Remember, many of these exams are designed to be challenging. Needing multiple attempts doesn't reflect on your intelligence or potential.

The Power of Resilience

Building resilience is key to long-term career success. Here are some strategies:

1. *Develop a Growth Mindset.* View challenges as opportunities to learn and improve.

2. *Practice Self-Reflection.* Regularly assess your experiences, both positive and negative, for lessons.

3. *Build a Support Network.* Cultivate relationships with colleagues and mentors who can offer perspective during tough times.

4. *Maintain Work-Life Balance.* A fulfilling life outside work can provide perspective and support when facing professional challenges.

Real-World Examples

Many successful individuals have faced significant setbacks:

- J.K. Rowling was rejected by 12 publishers before Harry Potter was accepted.

- Steve Jobs was once fired from Apple, the company he co-founded.

- Michael Jordan was cut from his high school basketball team.

What sets these individuals apart is their resilience and ability to learn from setbacks.

Generational Perspectives

It's important to understand that different generations may approach setbacks differently. While you might feel the need to process your emotions, your Gen X manager may expect you to "brush it off" quickly.

> *Tip:* In the workplace, focus on asking for concrete advice on improvement rather than emotional support. Save deeper emotional processing for friends, family, or a mentor.

The "Fairness" Trap

It's human nature to feel that setbacks are "unfair," but this mindset can be counterproductive. What feels unfair to you may be a well-reasoned decision based on factors you're not aware of.

Instead of dwelling on fairness, focus on what you can control:

1. Your performance in your current role.

2. Your efforts to develop new skills.

3. Your attitude and resilience in the face of challenges.

Career Progression Conversations

If you were passed over for a promotion, you may want to have a discussion with your boss about your career path. When discussing career advancement:

1. *Prepare.* Clearly articulate your career goals and what you want to learn.

2. *Ask for Guidance.* Seek your manager's perspective on your next steps and readiness.

3. *Show Commitment.* Emphasize your dedication to your current role while expressing interest in growth.

> *Tip:* Try this approach: "I'm committed to excelling in my current role, but I'm also eager to grow. Could we discuss potential next steps in my career and any skills I should be developing?"

Conclusion

Mistakes, failures, and setbacks are not roadblocks; they're detours on your career journey. By approaching them with resilience, a growth mindset, and a willingness to learn, you can turn these challenges into opportunities for development and eventually, success.

Story Summary

- Everyone makes mistakes; the key is handling them effectively through a five-step process: fix, inform, solve, learn, and improve.

- Career paths aren't always linear; patience and skill development are crucial when facing setbacks.

- Professional exam failures require self-reflection, analysis, and persistence.

- Many successful individuals, like J.K. Rowling and Steve Jobs, overcame significant setbacks.

- Generational differences exist in handling setbacks; focus on seeking concrete advice in the workplace.

- Avoid the "it's not fair" mindset and instead focus on what you can control.

- Approach career progression conversations with preparation, seeking guidance, and showing commitment to your current role.

Remember, your response to challenges is a key factor in your professional growth. Embrace these experiences as opportunities to demonstrate your resilience, adaptability, and commitment to continuous improvement.

Getting Ahead

Chapter 22

Understanding and Leveraging Your Professional Brand

In the workplace, your professional brand is not just a buzzword—it's the collective impression you make and the value you're known for. Think of it as your professional reputation, carefully cultivated and consistently demonstrated. But what exactly is this brand, and how do you use it without coming across as a self-promoter?

Let's break it down.

What Is Your Professional Brand?

Your professional brand is the unique combination of skills, experiences, and personality that you want to be known for in the workplace. It's not about creating a false image, but about consistently showcasing your authentic strengths and values.

Key components of your brand might include:

1. Your area of expertise (e.g., data analysis, creative problem-solving).
2. Your work style (e.g., detail-oriented, collaborative).

3. Your key strengths (e.g., meeting deadlines, innovative thinking).

4. The unique perspective you bring to your role.

> *Tip:* Reflect on what you want to be known for professionally. What do you want colleagues to think of when they hear your name?

How to Use Your Professional Brand

Using your brand isn't about constantly talking about yourself. Instead, it's about consistently demonstrating your value through your actions and communications. Here's how:

1. *In Your Work.* Consistently deliver on the key aspects of your brand. If you want to be known for creativity, consistently bring creative solutions to problems. Volunteer for projects that align with your brand strengths.

2. *In Meetings.* Contribute insights that reflect your expertise. Ask thoughtful questions that demonstrate your engagement and understanding.

3. *In One-on-One Interactions.* Share relevant experiences or knowledge that could help a colleague. Offer to assist on projects where your strengths could be valuable.

4. *In Performance Reviews.* Highlight accomplishments that reinforce your brand. Discuss goals that align with your professional brand and benefit the company.

5. *In Your Digital Presence.* Ensure your LinkedIn profile reflects your professional brand. Share or comment on industry-relevant content that aligns with your expertise.

Communicating Your Brand Without Bragging

The key is to let your work speak for itself while also ensuring your contributions are recognized. Here's how:

1. *Focus on Impact.* Instead of saying "I'm a great problem-solver," say "I enjoyed finding a solution to X problem, which resulted in Y improvement."

2. *Share Credit.* Acknowledge team efforts while highlighting your specific contribution.

3. *Ask for Feedback.* This shows you're committed to growth and gives others a chance to recognize your strengths.

4. *Offer Help.* Volunteer your skills in areas where you excel. This naturally showcases your strengths without explicit self-promotion.

Avoiding Common Pitfalls

1. *Overstatement.* Be careful not to exaggerate your role or the impact of your work, especially early in your career.

2. *Inconsistency.* Ensure your actions align with the brand you're trying to build. If you claim to be detail-oriented, don't submit work with errors.

3. *Lack of Awareness.* Understand how your role fits into the larger organizational context. Recognize that as a young professional, your projects may not yet have company-wide impact.

Evolving Your Brand

As you grow in your career, your brand should evolve:

1. *Seek Regular Feedback.* Understand how others perceive you and your work.

2. *Adapt to New Responsibilities.* As you take on new roles, ensure your brand reflects your expanding capabilities.

3. *Stay True to Your Values.* While your skills may change, your core professional values should remain consistent.

Conclusion

Your professional brand isn't something you announce—it's something you consistently demonstrate. It's the promise of value you bring to every interaction and project. By understanding and thoughtfully managing your brand, you position yourself not just for your current role, but for future opportunities and growth.

Story Summary

- Your professional brand is the unique value and strengths you consistently bring to your work.

- It's demonstrated through your actions, not just your words.

- Use your brand by consistently delivering on your key strengths and volunteering for aligned projects.

- Communicate your brand by focusing on impact and sharing credit.

- Avoid overstating your contributions, especially early in your career.

- Evolve your brand as you grow, always staying true to your core professional values.

Remember, building a strong professional brand is a career-long journey. It's not about creating a false image or constantly talking about yourself. Instead, it's about consistently delivering value and ensuring that your unique strengths are recognized and utilized in the workplace.

Chapter 23

Career Ownership: Networking, Mentorship, and Sponsorship

In the grand game of your career, networking, mentorship, and sponsorship are your power plays. They're not just buzzwords or optional extras—they're essential strategies for career growth and resilience. This chapter will demystify these concepts and show you how to leverage them effectively.

The Networking Imperative

Networking isn't about collecting business cards at awkward mixers. It's about building genuine, mutually beneficial relationships over time. Think of it as professional friendship-building.

Real-World Examples:

Zoe, a Gen Z professional, approached her job search strategically. She set up coffee meetings with everyone in her network, explaining her skills and career goals. At each meeting, she asked for advice and referrals to others. Within a month, she had a new job.

In contrast, Emily relied solely on online applications. After submitting over 100 resumes and enduring a lengthy, stressful process, she eventually found a position.

The lesson? Networking isn't just more effective—it's often more enjoyable and can lead to unexpected opportunities.

Networking Strategies

1. *Give to Get.* Offer help, share interesting articles, make introductions. Build goodwill before you need it.

2. *Stay Connected.* Regular check-ins keep relationships warm. A quick coffee or video chat can work wonders.

3. *Be Genuine.* Focus on building real connections, not just expanding your contact list.

4. *Leverage Technology.* Use LinkedIn and other platforms to stay connected and showcase your expertise.

Tip: After meeting someone new, follow up within 24 hours with a personalized message referencing your conversation.

Mentorship: Your Career Guide

A mentor is like a career sherpa, helping you navigate professional challenges. They offer advice, share experiences, and provide perspective.

How to Find a Mentor:

1. Identify potential mentors within and outside your organization.

2. Approach them respectfully, explaining why you value their guidance.

3. Be clear about what you're seeking—occasional advice or regular check-ins.

Remember, mentorship isn't one-size-fits-all. You might have different mentors for various aspects of your career.

Tip: Come prepared for mentorship meetings with specific questions or challenges to discuss.

Sponsorship: Your Career Advocate

While mentors advise, sponsors advocate. They're influential figures who champion your career, recommending you for opportunities and promotions. Importantly, sponsorship often involves mutual benefit, so it's essential to show how your success can reflect positively on your sponsor as well.

Attracting Sponsors

1. *Excel in Your Role.* Consistently deliver high-quality work that reflects well on your team and leaders.

2. *Be Visible.* Ensure key players know about your contributions and how they align with organizational goals.

3. *Express Your Ambitions.* Let potential sponsors know your career goals and how they tie into the company's success.

4. *Support Others.* Demonstrate your leadership potential by helping colleagues and contributing to a positive work environment.

5. *Deliver Results.* Consistently prove your capabilities by achieving or exceeding your goals. This allows potential sponsors to see how your work directly benefits them and the organization.

Remember, you don't typically ask someone to be your sponsor. You earn sponsorship through your performance, potential, and ability to create value for others.

Building Your Personal Board of Directors

Think of your professional relationships as a personal board of directors. Aim for diversity in experience, industry, and perspective. This might include:

1. A senior leader in your field.

2. A peer in a different department or company.

3. An expert in a skill you want to develop.

4. Someone from a completely different industry for fresh perspectives.

Overcoming Common Obstacles

- *Fear of Imposing.* Most people are flattered when asked for advice. You're not bothering them—you're valuing their expertise.

- *Feeling Inauthentic.* Networking isn't about being fake. It's about genuinely connecting over shared professional interests.

- *Introversion.* Networking doesn't always mean large events. One-on-one coffees or small group discussions can be equally valuable.

The Long-Term Perspective

Career ownership is a lifelong journey. Your network should evolve as you grow:

- *Early Career*: Focus on building a broad network and finding mentors.

- *Mid-Career*: Start thinking about sponsorship and becoming a mentor yourself.

- *Senior Level:* Leverage your network to drive organizational goals and support emerging talent.

Giving Back

As you progress, look for opportunities to mentor and sponsor others. It's not just altruistic—it enhances your leadership skills and expands your influence.

Measuring Impact

Regularly assess your professional relationships:

1. Are you maintaining a diverse network?

2. Do you have mentors who challenge and support you?

3. Are you positioning yourself to attract sponsors?

Set goals for relationship-building, just as you would for other aspects of your career.

Conclusion: Your Network, Your Career Capital

Your network, mentors, and sponsors form a crucial part of your career capital. They provide support, open doors, and offer perspectives you might not gain otherwise. Remember, these relationships are not transactional—they're about mutual growth and support over the long term.

By actively managing these relationships, you're not just advancing your career; you're enriching your professional life and contributing to a supportive work culture for everyone.

Story Summary

- Networking is about building genuine, mutually beneficial relationships.

- Mentors provide guidance, while sponsors advocate for your career advancement.

- Build a diverse "personal board of directors" for varied perspectives.

- Overcome networking fears by focusing on authentic connections.

- Career ownership is a lifelong journey—evolve your network as you grow.

- Give back by mentoring and sponsoring others as you advance.

- Regularly assess and set goals for your professional relationships.

Remember, in the world of work, no one succeeds alone. Your network is not just a safety net—it's a launchpad for your aspirations and a support system for your journey. Invest in it consistently, and it will pay dividends throughout your career.

Chapter 24

The Non-Linear Career Path: Navigating the Corporate Maze

If you've pictured your career as a straight ladder to the top, it's time to reimagine that journey. In today's dynamic work environment, careers often resemble a maze more than a ladder. This chapter will guide you through the twists and turns of a non-linear career path, showing you how to turn unexpected detours into opportunities for growth.

The Myth of the Straight Path

The idea of a straight, upward career trajectory is largely a relic of the past. Consider these Real-World Examples:

1. John Legend, before becoming a celebrated musician, started his career as a management consultant at Boston Consulting Group after graduating from the University of Pennsylvania.

2. Ava DuVernay, the acclaimed filmmaker, started her career in journalism and public relations.

3. Jonah Peretti, the founder of BuzzFeed and co-founder of The Huffington Post, began his career as a middle school computer science teacher before transitioning to digital media.

These individuals didn't climb a career ladder – they navigated a complex maze of opportunities, each step building towards their ultimate success.

The Reality of Modern Careers

Studies show that the average person changes jobs 12 times during their career, according to the Bureau of Labor Statistics. This isn't a sign of failure – it's an opportunity for growth and exploration.

Understanding the Non-Linear Path

A non-linear career path involves lateral moves, role changes, and sometimes even industry shifts. Each move builds your skill set, expands your network, and provides new perspectives.

Benefits:

1. Diverse skill set.

2. Broader network.

3. Increased adaptability.

4. Deeper understanding of business operations.

Taking Ownership of Your Career

Remember, you're the owner of your career. No employer will plan your path for you. Here's how to take control:

1. Self-reflect regularly on your interests and values.

2. Set both short-term and long-term goals.

3. Seek out learning opportunities, even outside your current role.

4. Build relationships across your organization and industry.

Types of Career Moves

1. *Lateral Moves.* These can provide new skills and perspectives. Don't dismiss them as "sideways" steps – they're often the key to future advancement.

2. *Upward Moves.* When you're consistently exceeding expectations and seeking more responsibility, it might be time for a promotion.

3. *Creation Moves.* Sometimes, the perfect role doesn't exist yet. Look for organizational needs that match your skills and propose new positions.

Creating Your Career Plan

1. Assess your skills, interests, and values.

2. Research roles and industries that align with your assessment.

3. Set SMART goals (Specific, Measurable, Achievable, Relevant, Time-bound).

4. Develop action steps to achieve these goals.

5. Regularly review and adjust your plan.

Working with Management

Involve your manager in your career planning:

1. Schedule regular career discussions.

2. Share your goals and ask for feedback.

3. Seek opportunities to develop new skills within your current role.

Leveraging Mentorship

A mentor can provide invaluable guidance in navigating your career maze:

1. Seek advice on potential moves.

2. Gain insights into different roles or departments.

3. Learn from their career journey and decisions.

Evaluating Opportunities

When presented with a new opportunity, consider:

1. Does it align with your long-term goals?

2. What new skills or experiences will it provide?

3. How does it fit into your overall career narrative?

Remember, it's okay to say no to opportunities that don't align with your goals. However, be mindful of the potential impact on relationships, especially with sponsors.

Tip: If declining an opportunity, express gratitude, explain your reasoning, and reaffirm your commitment to your current role or alternative growth paths.

Overcoming Challenges

1. *Imposter Syndrome.* Remember, feeling out of your depth in a new role is normal. Focus on learning and growth rather than perfection.

2. *Adaptability.* Each role or company may have a different culture. Stay open-minded and flexible.

Telling Your Story

A non-linear career path can be a significant asset in your professional journey. When crafting your resume, use the introduction or summary section to highlight how your diverse experiences have contributed to a unique skill set. In interviews, when asked about your career changes or why you want a particular job, emphasize how each role has built upon the last, creating a rich tapestry of skills and insights that make you an ideal candidate.

The Gen Z Perspective

As a Gen Z professional, you're entering the workforce with high ambitions and possibly significant economic challenges. The desire for rapid advancement is understandable, especially given factors like student debt and rising living costs. However, it's crucial to balance this ambition with realistic expectations and a long-term perspective.

Remember:

1. Skill acquisition often trumps titles in long-term career growth.

2. Lateral moves can lead to bigger leaps later.

3. Your diverse experiences are an asset in a rapidly changing job market.

Embracing the Journey

A non-linear career path isn't about aimless wandering – it's about strategic exploration. Each role is an opportunity to learn, grow, and refine your career direction. By staying curious, adaptable, and proactive, you can turn the corporate maze into an exciting journey of professional discovery.

Story Summary

- Careers often resemble mazes more than ladders.

- The average person changes jobs 12 times during their career.

- Non-linear paths offer benefits like diverse skills and broader networks.

- Take ownership of your career through self-reflection and goal setting.

- Consider lateral moves, upward moves, and creating new roles.

- Involve your manager and mentors in your career planning.

- Evaluate opportunities based on your long-term goals.

- Frame your non-linear path as an asset in interviews and on your resume.

- Balance Gen Z ambition with realistic expectations and a long-term perspective.

- Embrace the journey of professional discovery.

Remember, in navigating your career maze, there's no wrong turn – only new opportunities to learn and grow. Stay open to possibilities, and you might find your most rewarding path is one you never expected.

Chapter 25

The Art of Negotiation

In your professional journey, you'll encounter numerous situations that require negotiation skills. Whether you're discussing salary, project budgets, contract terms, or resolving conflicts with coworkers, the ability to negotiate effectively can significantly impact your career success. This chapter will equip you with the tools to navigate these conversations skillfully.

Why Negotiation Matters

Negotiation isn't just for high-stakes business deals. It's a daily part of professional life:

1. *Salary and Promotions.* Advocating for your worth and career advancement.

2. *Contracts.* Ensuring fair terms that benefit all parties.

3. *Budgeting.* Securing resources for your projects and ideas.

4. *Conflict Resolution.* Finding mutually agreeable solutions with colleagues.

Learning these skills early in your career, when the stakes are relatively lower, sets you up for success in more significant negotiations later.

Fundamental Principles of Negotiation

Two seminal works offer valuable insights into effective negotiation:

"Getting to Yes" by Roger Fisher and William Ury emphasizes principled negotiation:

1. Separate the people from the problem.

2. Focus on interests, not positions.

3. Generate options for mutual gain.

4. Use objective criteria.

"Crucial Conversations" by Patterson, Grenny, McMillan, and Switzler offers strategies for high-stakes discussions:

1. Start with heart (focus on what you really want).

2. Learn to look (be attuned to how you're reacting and how others are responding).

3. Make it safe (step out of the content of the debate to restore safety).

4. Master your stories (exert positive influence on your emotions).

5. State your path (share your facts, tell your story, ask for others' paths, talk tentatively, encourage testing).

6. Explore others' paths (listen, ask, mirror to confirm feelings, paraphrase, prime).

7. Move to action (decide how you'll decide, document decisions and follow up).

Preparing for Negotiation

Successful negotiation starts with thorough preparation:

1. *Define Your Objectives.* Know what you want and why.

2. *Research.* Gather relevant data to support your position.

3. *Understand the Other Party.* Anticipate their needs and concerns.

4. *Know Your BATNA.* Determine your Best Alternative to a Negotiated Agreement.

Negotiation Strategies

1. *Seek Win-Win Outcomes.* Look for solutions that benefit all parties.

2. *Create Value.* Explore ways to "expand the pie" before dividing it.

3. *Use Objective Criteria.* Base arguments on fair standards or expert opinions.

Emotional Intelligence in Negotiation

Emotions play a crucial role in negotiations. Developing your emotional intelligence can give you a significant advantage:

1. *Self-Awareness.* Recognize your own emotions and how they affect your negotiation style.

2. *Self-Regulation.* Manage your emotions, especially in tense situations.

3. *Empathy.* Understand and respond to the emotions of others.

4. *Relationship Management.* Build rapport and trust with your negotiation partners.

> *Tip:* Before entering a negotiation, take a moment to center yourself. Deep breaths can help manage anxiety and improve focus.

Communication Skills

Effective communication is the backbone of successful negotiation:

1. *Active Listening.* Focus on understanding, not just responding.

2. *Asking Questions.* Use open-ended questions to gather information and clarify points.

3. *Clear Articulation.* Express your ideas and needs clearly and concisely.

Handling Difficult Situations

Not all negotiations will be smooth sailing. Here's how to handle challenges:

1. *Aggressive Negotiators.* Stay calm and focused on the issues, not the person.

2. *Impasses.* Take a break, revisit interests, or bring in a mediator if necessary.

3. *Power Imbalances.* Focus on objective criteria and mutual interests.

Cultural Considerations

In our global workplace, be aware of cultural differences in negotiation styles:

1. Research cultural norms before international negotiations.

2. Be patient and open to different communication styles.

3. When in doubt, ask for clarification to avoid misunderstandings.

Technology and Negotiation

As remote work becomes more common, virtual negotiations are increasing:

1. Ensure a stable internet connection and familiar with the platform.

2. Pay extra attention to non-verbal cues in video calls.

3. Use shared documents for real-time collaboration on terms.

Ethical Considerations

Maintaining integrity in negotiations is crucial for long-term professional success:

1. Be honest and transparent.

2. Honor commitments made during negotiations.

3. Seek fair outcomes, not just personal gain.

Continuous Improvement

Every negotiation is a learning opportunity:

1. Reflect on your performance after each negotiation.

2. Seek feedback from trusted colleagues or mentors.

3. Stay updated on new negotiation techniques and strategies.

Conclusion

Negotiation is a skill that improves with practice. By starting early in your career, you're investing in an ability that will serve you well throughout your professional life. Remember, the goal isn't to "win" at all costs, but to find solutions that create value for all parties involved.

Story Summary

- Negotiation skills are crucial in various workplace scenarios.

- Fundamental principles include focusing on interests, not positions.

- Preparation is key: know your objectives, research, and understand the other party.

- Emotional intelligence plays a significant role in successful negotiations.

- Effective communication, including active listening, is essential.

- Be prepared to handle difficult situations and cultural differences.

- Virtual negotiations require additional considerations.

- Maintain ethical standards in all negotiations.

- Continuously improve your negotiation skills through reflection and practice.

By mastering the art of negotiation, you're not just advancing your own career — you're contributing to a more collaborative and productive work environment for everyone. Embrace each negotiation as an opportunity to learn, grow, and create value.

Chapter 26

Understanding the Company's Financials: Your Key to Strategic Thinking

As a young professional, you might wonder why you need to understand your company's financials, especially if you're not in a finance role. The truth is, financial literacy is your secret weapon for strategic thinking and career advancement. It's not just about knowing what your company does or what products it sells; it's about understanding how money moves through the organization and drives decision-making.

Why Financial Literacy Matters

Understanding financials helps you:

1. Speak the language of leadership.

2. Make informed decisions that benefit the company.

3. Identify opportunities for innovation and growth.

4. Contribute meaningfully to strategic discussions.

Remember, at publicly traded companies, pleasing shareholders with strong quarterly results and stock prices is a constant priority. Your ability to connect your work to these financial outcomes can set you apart.

How Money Moves Through a Company

At its simplest, a business takes in money (revenue), spends money (costs), and hopefully has something left over (profit). But the reality is more complex:

1. Revenue comes from sales of products or services.

2. Costs include everything from raw materials to salaries.

3. Profits can be reinvested in the business or distributed to shareholders.

4. Cash flow doesn't always match profitability (you can be profitable on paper but short on cash).

Understanding this flow helps you see how your role contributes to the bigger picture.

Key Financial Concepts

Even if you didn't study accounting, you can grasp these essential ideas:

1. *Revenue.* Money earned from sales.

2. *Costs.* Money spent to run the business.

3. *Profit.* What's left after subtracting costs from revenue.

4. **Assets.** What the company owns.

5. **Liabilities.** What the company owes.

6. **Equity.** The value of the company to its owners.

7. **Cash Flow.** The actual movement of money in and out of the business.

The Finance Department: More Than Just Number Crunchers

Understanding the roles in finance helps you collaborate more effectively:

- Chief Financial Officer (CFO): Oversees all financial operations.

- Controller: Manages accounting and financial reporting.

- Financial Analyst: Analyzes financial data to inform decision-making.

- Treasurer: Manages the company's cash and investments.

Your department likely interacts with finance for budgeting, expense approvals, or performance reporting. Knowing their perspective can smooth these interactions.

Public vs. Private Companies

Public companies face unique pressures:

- Quarterly earnings reports can drive short-term decision-making.

- Stock prices fluctuate based on financial performance and market perception.

Private companies might focus more on long-term growth and profitability without the scrutiny of public markets.

Connecting Your Role to Financial Performance

No matter your position, your work impacts the bottom line:

- Sales roles directly drive revenue.

- Operations roles often focus on controlling costs.

- Product development can impact both revenue and costs.

- Even support roles like HR or IT contribute to overall efficiency and profitability.

Understanding these connections helps you make decisions that align with company goals.

Building Your Financial Literacy

Start small:

1. Review your company's annual report or financial statements.

2. Ask questions when financial terms come up in meetings.

3. Offer to help with your department's budgeting process.

Remember, it's okay to not understand everything at first. The goal is continuous learning.

Conclusion: Financial Understanding as a Career Accelerator

Financial literacy isn't just for the accounting department. It's a powerful tool that can accelerate your career by helping you think strategically, communicate effectively with leadership, and make informed decisions. As you grow in your career, your financial acumen will become an increasingly valuable asset.

Story Summary

- Financial literacy is crucial for strategic thinking and career advancement.

- Understanding how money moves through a company helps you see the bigger picture.

- Key financial concepts include revenue, costs, profit, assets, liabilities, and cash flow.

- The finance department plays various roles that impact the entire organization.

- Public companies face unique pressures related to quarterly results and stock prices.

- Your role, regardless of department, impacts the company's financial performance.

- Building financial literacy is an ongoing process that starts with curiosity and asking questions.

Remember, becoming financially literate is a journey, not a destination. Start small, stay curious, and watch as your understanding of the business world expands

Getting Started

Chapter 27

Closing Thoughts

As you reach the end of this book, thank you for coming along on this journey. We hope the information has resonated with you. Our aim was to provide actionable strategies and clarity as you navigate the complexities of the modern workplace.

It's worth remembering that your professional journey is uniquely yours. Alongside your technical skills, you bring a perspective, creativity, and resilience that only you possess. Each of these qualities holds transformative potential in the workplace. We encourage you to use this book as a resource—return to it when you encounter challenges, and let it serve as a companion over time.

As we close, know that the game of navigating work-life balance, ambition, and well-being is ongoing. Every experience, conversation, and project will shape your approach at work which will help you become not only a valuable professional but a trusted colleague and leader.

Thank you for reading, and best of luck in everything you pursue.

About the Authors

Ellen Raim

Ellen Raim, the founder of ADOY, specializes in advising young professionals on navigating their early careers and supporting organizations in fostering and retaining Gen Z talent. With a unique blend of HR expertise and executive experience in C-suite roles, Ellen provides practical, empathetic strategies for both individual and organizational success. Her background in law, behavioral economics, and organizational design drives her people-first approach to workplace challenges and solutions.

Marcia Homer

Marcia Homer's career spans years in corporate Human Resources, where she has served as both a leader and a trusted business partner. With degrees in Human Resources, Social Sciences, and Applied Exercise Science, Marcia combines a deep understanding of human behavior with an approachable, candid style. Known for her talent in solving complex work issues and advocating for employee well-being, Marcia co-founded ADOY to empower young professionals to thrive independently in the workplace.

For further resources, guidance, or to reach out with questions, please visit our website at adoy.co. We'd love to hear from you—whether you have feedback, want to share your experiences, or are simply seeking advice. Remember, you're not alone in your career journey. We're here to support you as you continue to learn, grow, and play the game.

Resources

Below are additional explanations of the models discussed earlier in this book as well as citations to the original work.

SCARF Model

The SCARF model, discussed in chapter 10, was developed by Dr. David Rock. It identifies five key social domains that influence human behavior in collaborative settings: Status, Certainty, Autonomy, Relatedness, and Fairness. Understanding these domains helps leaders create environments that enhance engagement and reduce threats. The model is based Rock's neuroscience research and is widely used in organizational development and leadership training. Dr. Rock is the founder of the NeuroLeadership Institute, which focuses on applying neuroscience to improve leadership and workplace practices.

Rock, D. (2008). SCARF: *A brain-based model for collaborating with and influencing others. NeuroLeadership Journal*, 1, 44–52.

The Eisenhower Matrix

The Eisenhower Matrix, discussed on page 100, is sometimes referred to as the Urgent-Important Matrix. It helps individuals prioritize tasks by categorizing them based on urgency and importance. The four quadrants of the matrix are: (1) urgent and important—work that requires immediate attention, (2) important but not urgent—to be scheduled for later, (3) urgent but not important—these can be delegated, and (4) neither urgent nor important—minimize or eliminate.

This model is attributed to President Dwight D. Eisenhower, who was known for his productivity and decision-making skills. While there isn't a specific publication by Eisenhower detailing this model, the concept was popularized by Stephen R. Covey in his book: Covey, S. R. (1989). *The 7 habits of highly effective people: Powerful lessons in personal change.* New York, NY: Free Press.

Pareto Principle (80/20 Rule)

The Pareto Principle outlined on page 110, is also known as the 80/20 Rule. It states that roughly 80% of a project's impact results from 20% of the efforts. This principle is used in business and productivity contexts to identify the most important tasks on which to focus. The principle was introduced by Italian economist Vilfredo Pareto, who observed that 80% of Italy's land was owned by 20% of the population. He documented this concept in his work: Pareto, V. (1896). *Cours d'économie politique.* Lausanne: F. Rouge.

Pomodoro Technique

The Pomodoro Technique is a time management method that encourages focused work sessions followed by short breaks. The technique involves working for 25 minutes (a "Pomodoro" session) and then taking a 5-minute break. After completing four Pomodoros, a longer break of 15-30 minutes is taken. This approach helps maintain concentration and prevent burnout. Francesco Cirillo developed the method in the late 1980s. The "Pomodoro Technique" is named after the Italian word "pomodoro" which means "tomato," as the creator of the technique, Francesco Cirillo, used a tomato-shaped kitchen timer to set his focused work intervals, hence the name. Cirillo fully describes it in his book: Cirillo, F. (2006). *The Pomodoro Technique*. Penguin Random House LLC. New York, NY

RACI Model

The RACI model, mentioned on page 116, is a tool used in project management to clarify roles and responsibilities. RACI stands for Responsible, Accountable, Consulted, and Informed. Each task or deliverable in a project is assigned these roles to ensure clear communication and prevent confusion. "Responsible" refers to those who do the work, "Accountable" is the person who ensures the task is completed, "Consulted" are those whose input is sought, and "Informed" are those who need to be updated on progress. A detailed explanation can be found in: Project Management Institute. (2017). *A guide to the project management body of knowledge (PMBOK® Guide)* (7th ed.). Newtown Square, PA

Leaders Who Persevered

These anecdotes are found on page 142.

J.K. Rowling's Rejections: J.K. Rowling's manuscript for *Harry Potter and the Philosopher's Stone* was reportedly rejected by 12 publishers before being accepted by Bloomsbury.

Economic Times. (2023, July 27). *When Harry Potter was rejected by 12 publishers*. https://economictimes.indiatimes.com/magazines/panache/from-an-impoverished-single-mom-to-worlds-richest-writer-a-look-at-jk-rowlings-incredible-journey/when-harry-potter-was-rejected-by-12-publishers/slideshow/102276515.cms

Steve Jobs's Departure from Apple: In 1985, Steve Jobs was removed from his managerial role at Apple following internal conflicts and subsequently left the company he co-founded. ABC News. (2011, October 6). *When Steve Jobs got fired by Apple.* https://abcnews. go.com/Technology/steve-jobs-fire-company/story?id=14683754

Michael Jordan's Early Basketball Setback: A common anecdote is that Michael Jordan was cut from his high school varsity basketball team, which motivated him to improve. However, he was actually only placed on the junior varsity team. This experience did fuel his determination to excel. Lazenby, R. (2014). *Michael Jordan: The life.* Little, Brown and Company.

SMART Goals

SMART goals found on page 157, provide a framework for setting clear, achievable objectives. The acronym SMART stands for Specific, Measurable, Achievable, Relevant, and Time-bound. Each element ensures that goals are well-defined and actionable, making it easier to track progress and success. The concept was introduced by George T. Doran in his paper: Doran, G. T. (1981). *There's a S.M.A.R.T. way to write management's goals and objectives. Management Review,* 70(11), 35–36.

Getting to Yes by Roger Fisher

Getting to Yes discussed on page 164, presents a method for principled negotiation that focuses on mutual interests rather than positions. It outlines four key principles: separate the people from the problem, focus on interests--not positions, invent options for mutual gain, and insist on using objective criteria. This approach aims to produce fair agreements that maintain relationships. The book is a foundational text in negotiation and conflict resolution: Fisher, R., Ury, W., &

Patton, B. (1991). *Getting to yes: Negotiating agreement without giving in* (2nd ed.). New York, NY: Penguin Books.

Crucial Conversations by Patterson et al.

Crucial Conversations also explained on page 164, focuses on effective communication during high-stakes situations. The authors provide tools and strategies for handling emotionally charged conversations in a way that encourages open dialogue and mutual understanding. Key concepts include creating a safe environment for dialogue, mastering your emotions, and speaking persuasively without aggression. The book is widely used in leadership and organizational development: Patterson, K., Grenny, J., McMillan, R., & Switzler, A. (2002). *Crucial conversations: Tools for talking when stakes are high.* New York, NY: McGraw-Hill.